EDEN

IS NOW

THE ANSWERS YOU NEED TO LIVE
A JOYFUL LIFE ON EARTH
AND ASCEND IN PEACE

CHANNELED FROM EDEN

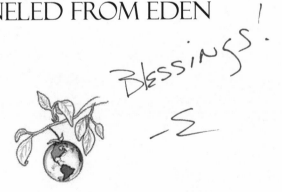

Blessings!
-E

An Earth Lodge® Publication
http://www.earthlodgebooks.com
Roxbury, Connecticut

This book contains valuable information, but it is not intended to take the place of proper medical care. Please seek qualified professional care for mental and physical health problems.

TABLE OF CONTENTS

A message for today?

Learn. Grow. Laugh.

WELCOME TO EDEN

Our name is Eden. Feel us, breathe us. We are what they call love, the burn of a thousand flames. We are as the mother, the great one, the one that creates: we watch a thousand souls flame to life and die and that has been in the space of a moment but we create them just as you do, you on your planet.

We are here and we want to you to ask questions. But we also want to tell you to walk in joy and without fear and to breathe breathe breathe when you feel you cannot.

We are all connected, we can see all, hear all, know all. Our teaching agenda is to enlighten you and those you know and those you do not yet know further and higher. We have agreed to come to you in this lifetime to teach you all we can about how to raise your vibration and increase your life span and your evolutionary potential. There are many things we also can talk to you about that are not directly related to these agendas for we are happy to answer all questions and all questions ultimately lead to the ONE. The one truth, one way, one reality.

Are you, and other source entities "non-returners" in the traditional Buddhist sense, who like Buddha achieved a certain level of enlightenment that they could go to "nirvana" after many lives and not return? Buddha decided to return and teach as a prophet, using his past lives as his form of teaching various virtues. The Buddhists believed that Christ was a prophet like Buddha. And the Muslims believe that Mohammed was the same...a prophet. Is this concept of non-returner the essence of what is called prophet? Did Kahlil Gibran channel the text of The Prophet from source entities like Eden and Abraham? Will some of these source entities come back to physical reality to be prophets, or simply to live another physical experience?

We are not all non-returners. If we were, our channels would not be on Earth, for they are connected to us, at one with them when they speak. Many souls advise prophets when they are on Earth, and many return. Often, we choose to do so to keep our knowledge and advice sound and current with your reality. Christ had many souls advising him, working together as his "higher self" when he was incarnated. Prophets are no better than other humans, the only difference is that they have remembered what they knew before they incarnated, or that they are able to hear their guides and greater, higher selves more clearly many humans.

YOUR LIFE PLAN

There are no requirements in this life. You can do whatever you desire. You can be or go whatever or wherever you want. Yes, your soul had some general ideas of the way it wanted to do things in this specific incarnation, but nothing you do can possibly be against your soul directive. You are completely free. Source places no limitations on the act of creation. None.

This is a big deal. This is a big truth. Really. NO limits.

Here in the physical wants and needs become distorted within the confines of time and material dynamics, so that it often seems as if you have limits, but truly you do not have a single one. And when a person on your plane of existence really gets that, well then, they do amazing things. And people call them gods, or ascended masters, or what have you. But they are just the same as you. They just have integrated fully with the concept that they have no limits. No miracles to small or big. No desires out of bounds or unattainable. Everything, for everyone, that they ever wanted.

So. There are things you are wanting to do, and what you are really wondering if they will distract you from your life's purpose, or from your true path. To that we have only one message, always one message. **Do what brings you joy**. If it makes you happy it is right. If it makes you happy, it is what your soul wants. If it makes you happy, you are lighting up a part of Source, and feeding the energy of the universe. When you are joyful, you are always in the right. You are always as you should be.

Sometimes, the things that bring you joy do not bring long lasting or extremely meaningful results. At least that is the way it feels to many of you, often. Sometimes the most joyful experience is planting a garden, or starting a new business, which then does not grow or flourish and is quickly abandoned. Were these things wastes of time? Did you fail? No. No they were not, and no you did not. Everything moment that brings you joy in its inception, whether successful or not in the end, is an important learning moment. It is a time of wondrous creation. It may simply be that you are working through something unconsciously before you can do something else. It may be that you simply needed to feel that moment of expansion, no matter how brief. The thing is, no joy is ever wasted. No desire happily met should ever be avoided. You will only be spreading yourself too thin if you put too much pressure on yourself. If you wish to begin a play, then simply sit down and write. If it begins, only to be put aside, or be written in fits and starts, there is no harm in that. Sometimes things take time. Everything has its season – it may time to begin a writing project, although the time to finish it is a decade away. Or you might find that writing a little every day becomes a form of meditation for you, a supremely relaxing and nourishing part of your day. Flow with it, and let your projects flow with you. Let your life flow in a stream of JOY.

LOVE

The greatest love story you will ever have, you could ever have, in this life or any other, is with your self. The greatest love connection you could ever have is with Source. These are the connections which need to be fostered, and then all other connections will naturally flow and align, all at the proper time and in the proper way.

From a vibrational standpoint, we see all souls are awash in love. All beings, at their core, love all beings. But on Earth, where the majority of the planetary beings are expressing judgement values as part of the creationary process, it is of course different. Often, one may love another, but not be able to be with that person, for a variety of reasons.

This is a time of a vast re-awakening of the heart chakra so that it can return to its divine original blueprint. With your heart chakras fully opening, telepathic abilities and other psychic sensitivities will re-emerge, as they are meant to. Each human who experiences this remembering sends a shock, a pulse, of love throughout the matrix of mass consciousness. Each pulse inspires other hearts to open, to remember, and to reintegrate.

Humanity was meant to exist in a state of open, unconditional love. Over eons, subjected to conflicts with other races and dimensions, the heart (along with the rest of humanity's DNA) became corrupted and distorted, so that the heart chakra folded in upon itself, unable to experience full and open love as it was meant to. Humanity can only return itself to its former glory and pure DNA patterning after its hearts have been resurrected.

Do not be afraid to love, or to live. Do not worry so much. You are YOU. Nothing can change that. Not the love of another, or the lack of love. You came here to live. Fear nothing. Nothing can harm you, for energy cannot be destroyed. Matter cannot be destroyed. You are pure light, love, and energy, and you should feel free to attract the same to yourself. Be STRONG and LOVE! Love it all. Life is love, as are you. Bathe in it. Good, beautiful things surround you. Appreciate them. Love them. List them. Enumerate them. Count them. Soon, you will see there are too many to count.

HEALING WITH THE I AM

Begin by meditating on the words "I am". Repeat them to yourself as a mantra for several minutes, followed by repetitions of:

I am light.
I am purity.
I am love.

Repeat until you feel buoyant and free. Then surround yourself with a sphere of white light. See this white light growing and encompassing your entire home. When you go to a work space or anywhere you will be sitting for a few minutes, including your car, including the beach, including restaurants or friends' homes, repeat the mantra, "I am light, I am purity, I am love," again and visualize the sphere of white light again, also expanding to protect the space. With repetition, this sphere of clarity and love will become part of your energetic signature so that spaces will be automatically cleared when you enter them.

INTENT

Intent, or will, is the most important thing you can learn in this lifetime. In any situation, your intent is always what will determine the outcome. When you are clear about what you want, and do not dwell on that which you do not want, you will always attract that which you do want. There is no difference between what you intend, or will, and what you receive. In terms of your love-match, you should be open and honest, just as you should in all aspects of your communication with all other beings, and not worry about forcing things or fighting against anything. That which you fight against, you only make stronger: far better then, for you to focus your intent and will upon that which you do want. Know what you want, and then allow yourself to receive it. Expect to receive it. Do not worry about how to make what you want happen. Just be clear in your heart about what you desire, and trust that the universe will help you manifest that desire in an easy and expedient manner. Do not focus on that which makes you unhappy. Do not participate in conversations which make you unhappy or fearfull. Change the direction of your thoughts and words towards the light, and the dark will recede. Do only those things that make you feel joy, love, and fulfillment, and you will soon see the world around you begin to change to meet your desires, and to bring you more joy.

Intent is everything. The strength of your will and the intention behind it is all that determines the outcomes of your ceremonies, rituals, prayers. If you believe that you need a particular construction, than you will. If you do not, than you don't. You create your reality. There is only your desire and will to take into consideration. If you need to do particular rituals to focus your intention, than by all means do them. Play with it. Enjoy it. The world is yours to do with as you will. Do not be beholden to another's world, or their will.

Every day on your planet is holy, and every moment is an opportunity for you to spread a message of love, or a message of fear. Which would you rather spread? Listen to your words. Every word you choose has power, every word changes the world around you with its energy, like a tiny stone tossed in a pond. Words of joy spread from person to person, snowballing, expanding, to change the entire world. Words of fear do the same thing. Which words will you speak this season? In your country of America right now, you are entering your most holy season of love, hope and belief in the power of innocence. Use the energy of the elements, of nature, to increase your own joy, and the joy of others.

When you are joy-full, you infect those around you with feelings of joy, and this joy spreads from person to person, growing and changing the world. Be that which you wish to see in the world.

MANIFESTATION

You absolutely want to be clear about what you want. When you do "ask" for something, when you pray or set your intention, be as clear as you possibly can about what you want and why you want it. Part of the asking is knowing why you are really asking for something. Do you want comfort? Companionship? Passion? A sense of belonging? A To reconnect with the closest member(s) of your soul group? Support? Excitement? A family unit? To resolve old karma? To move along clearly on your life path? What are you really asking for here? And why are you asking for it? This is a huge component of the asking, for the more clarity you deliver with your intention, the better the universe can co-create with you to bring you what you are asking for. Always set this intention with the clarity of purpose that it be for your highest good, and the highest good of all involved.

Once you have infused your intention with clarity of purpose and vision, know that you have already set your vision in motion. It is already on its way to you. It is easier to create a clear vision than it is to "tweak" it once it is already partially manifested. So be clear. And then, be easy.

Release your vision like a soap bubble, out into Source, and know that as all bubbles do, soon it will POP and be manifest in your world. It is always so, for it must be so. That is law. If people ask you what you are waiting for or how you are doing, remember this: You are well. You are on your true life path. You are following the signs that your higher self left for you. You are always in the right place, at the right time, doing exactly the right thing. And you will always be well. When in doubt, when you feel lonely or sad or wonder what is taking so long, do something that brings you joy. Follow your joy. Your joy is a sign from your soul that you are in the right place doing the right thing. Your sadness or worry is always a sign that you are not, that you are dwelling in a place of fear or low vibration and that you are enabling a disconnect from the flowing loving energy of Source. So be in joy. Be FULL of joy. Do what makes you happy, nurture your self, and remember – you are well.

You might wonder what you can do to move things along so that you can be more comfortable during the process.

The first thing we would like you to do is to set aside a day, or even just a few hours, to nurture yourself. Take some time for yourself. Do things that make you feel good, cared for. It can be day hiking and eating your favorite decadent foods, or just an evening of bathing with candles and scented oils, reading your favorite book and sipping hot chocolate. A morning of yoga and meditation, or a show at the movies. Whatever it is, take some time just for you, and do it alone. Spend some time with yourself, taking care of your self. After you have done that, we want you to sit down and think about what you would like to welcome into your life that would make you more comfortable in your body, more at ease on earth, more happy with your existence. Is it new clothes? Different foods? More time alone, or more time spent socializing? What sets you back, making you ill at ease, and what makes you feel good?

Think about those things. Make a list. Draw pictures. Make a vision board. Whatever you like to do, keep a record of what you find out about yourself. Next, we want you to look over your list and determine what it is that you are really wanting out of life right now. What is missing? What would bring you more joy on a daily basis? What does not? Here you have the root of what you are really wanting and needing, what things are really important to your soul path, and what you are not.

So often, people confuse abundance with what they are wanting, when in fact it is simply one way of getting there. So rather than focusing on the missing means, focus on what fuels your soul.

14

That is what will get you where you are wanting and needing to be.

CREATION

There is nothing that is out of reach for you. You can create anything you can conceive of. This is the truth of the gospels, this is the truth of the old prophets, and the perfection of God that is manifest in each and every one of you. Before anything can exist on the physical plane, it must first take shape and form in the astral, etheric planes. Having the idea is like planting a seed. It creates a blueprint for the form to manifest. But the seed must be watered – in the etheric realm this means dreams, planning, visualizing. Conceiving an idea is indeed just that – conception, a birthing process.

Close your eyes. Imagine yourself full of bliss and joy. See the circumstances that would surround you. Allow yourself to feel the fullness of this emotion, this utter happiness. Feel the light of Spirit flowing through you, and touching everything that you touch. You are surrounded by the love and the radiance of God, of Spirit. Isn't it wonderful? Allow yourself this full experience now, and you can recreate it anytime throughout your day. The more often you are filled with this perfect feeling of joy and love for life, the sooner and more often you will experience miracles flowing through your daily life. Miracles small, miracles large. Miracles of coincidence, of friendship, of peace. There are no miracles too hard to achieve. All are easy, for all possibilities are stored within every atom within every fiber of your being. Be easy. Be Blessed.

CO-CREATION

Elementals, guides, spirit – they all are happy to work on any creation that is done with good intention. People...this is not always so. Co-creation with other people is often more difficult than co-creation with elementals or Spirit. When you work with other people, the co-creative process necessitates a melding of vision. So in the melding, your vision gets changed. And the outcome changes. And if the person you work with is creating from a standpoint that is not with a heart then the reward from the universe is not as great. This is simplifying things a good deal, but you can see what we mean. So the co-creative process of creating abundance with another person is not the same as creating it on your own. In co-creation, the vibration of the process is created in such a way that $1+1=3$. Each vibration is magnified in co-creation. Whether it is a high vibration or a lower vibration. Everything happens faster, and not always in a "good" way. But part of your path on earth is to work on co-creation, so this is all part of the job description.

One thing that can serve any human team would be to have a short "dream session." At the beginning of any project sit together and brainstorm about creative ideas and how to progress with the project. Another session or two along the way that is less planning related and more visionary in scope can help clarify issues for people individually, as well as for the team, and keep the project on track. This could be done relaxed, friendly, round-table style, or by sending people home with a little writing questionnaire via email with focused questions regarding each team members vision or dream for the impact of the project and why it is important to them.

These questions will help you and the team in multiple ways, in particular:

It will show you, as team leader, what is really motivating people and how to help bring out their best work.

It will remind each person why they are doing this work, and what really matters.

If you think there is not time or appropriate atmosphere for a group meeting like this, or that they would not like the quick writing task, you also have the option of taking a different team member for lunch or coffee each day and conducting the session privately.

The only limit for your creative potential is the scale with which you co-create. This is to say, that you cannot do it alone. And yet you can. Ha ha let us explain! You begin with the intention and idea and focus. You have the drive and the passion. That is you, alone. Or is it? The best, largest, brightest, most passionate inspirations derive from a connection with source, so that the source connection, your full soul intention and master level intuition, comes down through you, into you, ready to be birthed into the physical. Then you begin to create. Sometimes the process works smoothly and easily. Sometimes it does not. Co-creation is a process of working not-alone that can both make projects flow more easily, or make one feel as if there are too many chefs in the kitchen. The best kind of co-creation begins when you open to your guides and the elementals, to mass-consciousness and the angels, to your higher self and the highest good, and you work in concert with the will of all to create the best possible outcome. That is co-creation at its finest. And with that kind of co-creation, you can make new worlds. With that kind of co-creation, you can create a star. With that kind of co-creation, you can alter the very flow of time.

CREATIVITY & HATHOR

The great mother goddess Hathor is an ultimate creator guide for humans. She is shown with two cow-horns on her head, and a sun disc between them. But this is not how these things were always known. She did not become associated with cows until much later in her god-hood, and yet the horns were always there. The horns are not animal parts, but are physical manifestations of the two-pronged approach to CREATION. These two prongs are WILL and INTENT. Without both, there can be no purposeful creation. The "sun disc" between them, is the manifested energy of creation as it takes form, as it *becomes*. It is a THOUGHTFORM, a thought or idea become reality. One way to help understand this is to visualize the exhibits at a science museum, where they show two metal rods inches apart, and send electricity up between them. Bzzt. It climbs back and forth, upwards between the rods and is released into the atmosphere. Bzzt. So it is with the act of purposeful creation. Thoughts are energy. Your thoughts, channeled up and out through the top of the head with strong will and directed intent, become reality. WILL + INTENT + THOUGHTFORM = CREATION.

CHANNELING

I've been trying to communicate with the light beings I feel I'm meant to connect with, but I don't know how. I've tried meditation and automatic writing and am wondering what else I can do. Sometimes, I think I'm feeling or hearing from one group or more, but then I lose whatever I feel I might have picked up. How can I connect with them more effectively?

We have heard you talking to us, late at night, early in the morning, as all times of day. All of source hears you and answers you. What we want to say is not so much that you are not connecting with us, but that you are not trusting the answering voice. When you are hearing us you are hearing us in your head, in your own voice. It feels so much like a part of yourself, so that you do not trust that you are receiving real, true channeled advice from Source, from Spirit. But you are. We talk to you all the time. Source, talks to you all the time. Your guides, talk to you all the time. All of creation is singing to you. And you are hearing us.

When you have a thought in your head that is pure mind, the thought feels like it comes from your entire head. When it is channeled, usually the thought will feel like it comes from just part of your brain. It will still "sound" like one of your own thoughts, but you will feel it just above your right ear, or just in your frontal lobe, or just at your crown, or somewhere else. You might also feel a pressure in that area, like someone is tapping you there or even squeezing your head. Sometimes, more rarely, you will actually hear someone speaking in your ear or near you, but this is more unusual.

Why do you hear us as if we are part of you, in your own voice? Because, you ARE part of us. And whose voice will you understand better, than your own? When we talk to you we use your vocabulary, your syntax, your grammar. We flow through you, so we speak as you. There can be no other way. When you see a channel struggling for the word to use in an explanation, it is not because we, Source, do not know all the words, but because we are filtering it through that particular mind's lexicon.

We are speaking to you. All you need to do is think a little less, focus a little less, and trust your own voice a little more. Then you will begin to realize that all along you have held the answers. All along you have known the way. You do not need to do deep meditation, although that is a wonderful way to feel as one will All-That-Is. You simply need to relax, and allow your mind to unfold, to release the controls, and be ready for what comes next.

All is well. You are a divine voice of God. You are one will all of creation, and creation is one with you.

FEAR

Fear! What is fear but the expectation of something bad that is going to happen to you? Do you not realize that your thoughts have magnificent powers? Do you not yet know that what you expect and believe is what you will create? Be not afraid. Be confident. Do not give in to those that would peddle fear among you. Be ever vigilant and ever joy-full in your knowledge and belief and EXPECTATION that the world is forever improving. You chose to be alive now so that you could experience vast improvements in the quality of life on Earth. Do you really believe that you are all failing? Do you really believe that you came here to help the world decline? Of course not. Your world is shifting, and things are changing. That which is no longer relevant will fall away, and that which is needed will improve. Do not fear this time of change, but be full of anticipation instead, for what new things will come. This is an EXCITING time! Be excited! You are all blessed, and all will be well. Do not believe anything else.

Dear Ones, you are so blessed. And most of you do not know it. Allow yourself to be an open receptacle for the energy of the universe. Open your whole self to Spirit. Why live in fear? Turn off your televisions. Turn off your newspapers. Turn off your computers. Turn off the gossiping, the fear-mongering. Live your life the way you want to live it. If you hunker down and live in fear and live as if disaster is coming, what do you think will happen? It is as if you are putting a big sign on your front door: "Disaster, come here! Party tonight!" Instead, invite in your blessings. Focus on the good in your life. Focus on the wonderful things you can buy, see and do every day. Turn your eyes and ears away from anything that makes you feel bad, and look to the light. Fill your heart with love, hope and laughter, and that is what will surround you.

Think back on your short history as humans. There is more peace on your planet now than you have seen for thousands of years. What are you so afraid of? As your mass consciousness aligns with Christ-consciousness, which we assure you it **is** doing, and you open more fully to love and joy, so your nervous systems also become more sensitized, and *aware* of when you are out of alignment with love and joy. And so, smaller disturbances create greater emotional upsets, which translate into societal instability and economic worries. But in **reality** humanity is, as a whole, much better off than it has been during its recent history. And conditions are continuing to improve every day. There is less war, less starvation worldwide, less disease, less fear. Yes, there are still many pockets of fear. But so much less. Put yourself in your races past, and then see your life from their perspective. You are **so** well, on a daily basis. You are living a dream. Be grateful, and be joyous. Release your worries. Live consciously, and do not allow other people to dictate what you should feel, fear, or believe.

There is nothing that your soul can not handle, and nothing that you must endure, for you are a limitless being made for joy and the interminable variety of life that is on earth. You can do everything you can think of. Everything. You are blessed beyond your wakeful imagination. Arise, humans, and claim your power! You are the most powerful force in your own existence. You can choose your reality and choose to live in fear, or live in wonder, awe and joy. When you live in wonder, everything that you create will be as a miracle to you, and there are no limits to what you can do. And when you live in fear you create misery out of anger, pain out of despair. Which would you rather do? Reclaim your humanity. Choose your true nature. Choose power. Live with your heart.

APATHY

Many people on the planet at this time are experiencing a lack of interest or a feeling of disassociation or detachment from all or part of their lives, to varying degrees. Why? Because you are all shifting. Many of you are quickly transitioning into a new era of being, a higher vibration and a new recognition of what you want and why you want it, and you want it now. As this is happening, some of you are merely experiencing the energetic separation from the old before the new emerges. This can feel strange and disconcerting. It is OK. Let go, and trust your self. Know that you will be taken of. Know that the new is coming. Know that everything you want, is coming. Your new life is, right now, aligning with your new energy pattern.

SADNESS

The very fact that you feel lost and down is a very clear indicator that you are not hearing or following your own guidance. If you are feeling down, then you are not in alignment with your true self. If you are sad or angry, your predominant thought pattern is in direct opposition to what your true self and your guides would have you do or feel: which is always, at its root, to BE IN JOY.

Everyone receives messages from their guides in a different manner. Some people hear voices, some people find small visual messages throughout the day (omens, or confirmations, such as hawks flying overhead when they have a certain thought, or the wind blowing just a bit harder at a particular moment, or a compelling ad on the TV.) Some people experience physical sensations such as a tap on their hand, or a tickle in their ear. And still others experience things in their gut, or just a simple "knowing". For all, though, the emotions are a powerful indicator which allow one to see when they are on the right path or not. If you cannot sustain happiness, then you are not on the right path. Period.

And when you are persisting in doing and thinking that which draw you away from your self, that which makes you unhappy and joy-less, then you are distancing yourself from your guides, from your guidance system. Remember that when you feel badly – uneasy, sick to your stomach, sad, upset – it is most often your soul's way of telling you that you are not in a good state of mind or being. It is a sign to look more closely at what you are believing or doing. If you are not happy, then you need to change the status quo.

So the first thing we would tell you is to do something that makes you feel better. Do something that makes you smile. And then do it again. And then ask yourself and your guides what you can do to keep that feeling. And do that. And do it again. Everything will be as it will be. Trust your self. Trust your joy.

When you are one with Spirit, and your light shines like a beacon to those around you. We would like to see you feel and enjoy your own light more, but we see that so many of you reading this are "empaths" and you are easily bogged down by the sadness of others around you, that another's heaviness can easily lower your own vibration and create feeling of disconnection with in you. We would like so much for this to happen less often, for it is not your true nature to be sad or heavy or depressed.

How can you shield your vibration from others in order to maintain your natural feelings of joy and gratitude for life on earth?

It is not necessary for you to remove your self from the presence of others who are lower in vibration or making you sad. You need only to remember that which makes you joy-FULL and spend more time doing that, more time being that, more time remembering that. The more joy-FULL you are, the harder it is for other emotions to fill you up. It is the **single** most important thing you can do to improve your private life, and your personal quality of *being*. When you are in joy and enjoying what you are doing, then all else naturally falls into alignment with that vibration, and feels and is well.

KINDNESS

Taking care of your self is not the same as being selfish. Making sure that you do what you love, with people you love, is not the same as being unloving. Making sure that you treat others kindly and demanding that you are treated the same is not the same as being unkind. It would be unkind, perhaps, to distance yourself from someone while saying words that are meant to wound, meant to make them feel bad, or words that are untrue. But when you stay true, say what you mean in a clear way, and are simply trying to remain heart-centered...no, of course you are not unkind. Don't ever think it. Loving someone does not mean you must always stay in the same space with them. Loving yourself makes it possible to love the world around you, and to receive that love tenfold in return.

STAYING ALIGNED

There are people around you that you feel sometimes make life very difficult, and even "bring you down." They have not been sent to you as a test, as you sometimes feel. Every person has the ability to be joyful or morose, mean or nice. Every person on earth is a being of light, no exceptions. And every person is a physical manifestation of energy: energy which can be connected or disconnected from source. Every person is constantly interacting with the energies around him or her, and responding on a cellular level to those energies. If you want the people around you to be greater reflections of the *light* then the easiest and quickest thing for you to do is to become a beacon of light yourself. Radiate light. Remain in the light. Shine nothing forth but light. There can be no dark where there is light. This will help the people around you remain connected to Source and behave in a manner more consistent with what you like, especially those that do not know how to connect to Source on a conscious level. Become a shining example.

No one can lower or raise your vibration except you: you must be responsible for your own connection to Source and the level of your own vibration. We know that it is not always easy. We know that there are many moments of frustration and disharmony for you, for all of you that are earthbound. But it needs to be that way. Begin with simple clearing exercises. Make sure you are grounded every day. There are crystals that can help (selenite, carnelian, fluorite, danburite, kyanite). Foods that are less processed allowed the body to remain more clear. Simple chakra clearing and alignment meditations or exercises are very good on a daily basis. Deep Breathing. Singing. Dancing. ALL things that bring you joy are instantly clearing and aligning, because you could not **be** joyfull if you were not clear and aligned.

You have all the power you need. You have all the power and magnificence of the universe at your fingertips, in your fingertips, in every cell of your body, and every ion of your soul. Harness your greatness. You are ONE with Source and Source is one with you. You are loved, and loved by all, for you ARE all, just as all IS you.

LIGHTING UP

Here is what we want you to do. Every moment of every day we want you to pay attention to how you are feeling. Does your action (or inaction) fill you up with light? Does it make you happy? If not, stop what you are doing and turn to something that does light you up. Yes, of course, sometimes you humans must do things you don't love, like taxes! But Trust us – if you are spending the majority of your time doing the right things at the right moment, even the completion of something as dreary or stressful as taxes can become a fulfilling, happy experience. Yes, it can and it does. SO. Do what brings you joy. Joy is a signal from your soul that you are on the right track. Fear, anxiety and stress are all signs that you are either doing the wrong things, or you are approaching them from the wrong angle or mindset.

It is not selfish to pursue your joy. You cannot do anyone any good if you are not filled up with light and happiness yourself. You'll soon be running on empty that way, and shutting down. So light yourself up. Fill yourself up. If there are tasks that must be completed that you are dreading, such as paperwork, etc, do something you really like first, or promise yourself (and deliver) a reward later. If you continue in this way, you will soon find yourself in the future, happy and fulfilled, and hardly any idea how you got there, because it was such an easy, happy process.

We do not get the sense that there are old vows of poverty blocking you, or anything like that. There are no grand rituals you need to do, other than the ritual of enthused, ebullient self-worship. Love yourself. Take care of yourself. Be there, now, for you. You need you.

THE PAST

When you dwell in the past, you are not in the present. The world into which you have incarnated is designed to move through time linearly, like a car. While you roll backwards, you cannot move forwards. You can not, either, remain parked and move forward. Moving forward, while continuously scanning your mirrors, is even more dangerous. Look ahead. Look to the sides. Pay attention to what your body and mind are doing.

We ask you, to please be here now. It is why you came. Courage, dear one. Courage. You can do this, we know it, and you know it. You knew it before you were born, and you know it deep in your soul. This life was *made* for you, because you made it. Every little piece of your life, you have made. If there are things you are yearning for, or missing, it is because you have neglected to make them whole, with all your intent and heart in them. Now, dear one, is the time for you to move forward. Allow your self to flow gently and easily with life. Say **"yes"** to everything. Be open to every opportunity. Be open to everything, joyfully, happily, blissfully accepting. The more you accept with a smile, the more you will receive.

Every moment that your heart is smiling "YES!" to the world, you are creating days and days of joyous bliss in your future. When you hunker down and want to hide your head and shake it "no", those are the moments that you are rejecting the days of bliss. It is time, now, to begin accumulating days, months and years of bliss.

ANCIENT KNOWLEDGE

Over many years of reading and researching, I find myself connected so much to the past, the bloodlines, the secrets of different cultures and societies, the ancient esoteric knowledge. Part is genetic memory, but part is likely soul memory. How useful is this information?

Through the research, you may come to see how it is all connected. You connect with other lifetimes, and it can help you complete the karmic and evolutionary lessons of those lives.

However, do not connect those lives together so that you could dwell in the details. Connect the lives together so that you can create an enhanced life experience, a bigger picture. The hidden knowledge, the secrets, are not important. They are fun, they are interesting, but they are not important. Certain bloodlines do carry an energetic imprint that has already been awakened, so that one born into the bloodline comes in with some of the work already done for them, so to speak, but it is nothing that every human cannot do themselves, bloodline or not. Being of certain bloodline has always given one a bit of a head start, especially at those times when most of humanity was living asleep at the wheel, but these days so many are awakened, so many are being born already free of karma, tapped in and turned on, that there is only a small advantage to being of any bloodline. The secrets in the past spoke of how to awaken the energies of the bloodline. Humanity, you included, are beyond these secrets now. You are awakened. **You do not need to focus on the sleeping times to better see an awakened future.**

So why would you bring all these times together, what was the point? The point was to see that there was a point! To come in knowing that the destination of humanity is evolution. That you are living so that you can grow. That every human life begins with growth, and should proceed that way every day - growing, expanding, becoming.

You have seen, in life after life, that love is the answer. That only love and compassion matter. **Judgment ends all being. Anger stifles growth. Fear creates disease.** These are the material lessons you learned during these times. You experimented to see if these emotional states could be accommodated within the human experience without harm, and they cannot. **Only love and compassion, tenderness and joy, can light the world spark.**

Love, and understand. Love, and be the culmination of your birthright, of your DNA.

Return to the beginning. To the Alpha, and be the Omega. Be the culmination of your own creation. Continue to live your plan, be an awakened being, and evolve.

TIME

Time begins to pass more quickly on your planet as there is less of a buffer between what you think and what you manifest or create. This buffer or lag of time existed so that you would be less likely to create those things which you did not mean to create consciously. With each new year of babes born on your planet, there are more and more children, and people, who remember what they came here to do, and how to go about deliberately creating it. Therefore, the need for a long lag time between when the thought to create occurs, and the manifestation of that thought occurs, is no longer needed. So many of you feel as though time is speeding up. Concurrently, some of you notice that while time seems to pass quickly, there are many days when everything you meant to accomplish, you do, in a shorter amount of time, and with more ease. This is also a manifestation of conscious and deliberate creation, for when you create consciously, the universe conspires to aid you. Things happen with ease. Life flows more easily.

Our message to you then, is to be joyous in your daily intents, to think only those thoughts which make you happy, and to then be joyous when those thoughts are manifested. When un-joyous thoughts manifest, do not despair, for joy is still but a thought, and a moment away. Focus on the joy, and the rest will un-manifest itself.

Mass consciousness has deemed time to be more flexible lately, and is allowing more manipulation of time in this century. This is because as the vibration of your species and your planet rises, the constrictions of time are no longer of as much benefit to your continued evolution. So, now, if you feel you need more time, just take a moment to think and to believe that you have all the time in the world, and time will pass more slowly for you while you need it to. Time can also speed up when you feel hurried or rushed, time reacts to meet your emotions and expectations of being rushed: so if you want to be un-rushed, be slow and easy and KNOW you have more time.

FAIRIES & NATURE DEVAS

I would like to work the fairies more closely. How can I do this?

Working with the fairies is little different from working with the angels, your guides, or various gods. You merely need to ask for assistance, and they will rise to the challenge. Fairies are part of the elements, of nature, and so they are all around you. With you, they were designed by Source to protect and nurture your physical reality. They are creative creatures, molding and directing energy on your plane at all levels, and so they are particularly well-suited to help you with manifesting your desires and dreams. They have no problem bringing creative thoughts into the physical realm as real and tangible results. So fear not, and have faith. That is the first requirement.

The second requirement to working with fairies is that you do not abuse the natural world. Pick up trash, be kind to plants and animals, do not waste resources or pollute.

To ask your local fairies for help, go outside, or position yourself near a houseplant or crystal. Call on the fairies and state what you are wanting, and ask for their assistance. If you are a friend of the fairies, a friend of nature, they will joyfully assist you. Leave the fairies a token of thanks, such as a shiny crystal or object, a floral candle, yummy treat (make sure you unwrap any candy or chocolate!) Then sit back, and allow yourself to believe that all will be well: that is your half of the work. If you feel the urge to do something nice for nature, do it right away: the fairies will be very appreciative: pick up trash on the road, donate money to an animal shelter, volunteer at a park. Soon you will see positive results.

DEVAS

Eden has mentioned that some orbs are guides and some are nature devas, but I do not really understand what a nature diva is. Is a nature diva the same as a fairy or gnome? If fairies and gnomes are different from nature divas, would Eden please explain what they are and how I could learn to see them? Do they have a role in our lives, if they exist, or are they simply living their own   lives?

Nature Devas are the elements, the creative energy of nature, that which keeps nature flowing and in flow. They work and play with the chi of the Earth, and they ARE the chi of the earth. They are many things. They keep the plants growing and the flowers flowering and the wind blowing and sometimes they ARE the wind and the plant and flowers. They work with the rocks and sometimes they ARE the rocks. Some powerful devas and groups of devas have named by humans GODS and NYMPHS and SYLPHS. Sprites and fairies.

Overlighting Devas protect you and the land, and help your plants grow free and strong.

"Overlighting" means that they watch over you, while simultaneously bringing more LIGHT to the area where they are.

Devas and angels watch over the land and the earth. They play with the wind and the trees, the skies and the waters. Devas are more intimately involved in the workings of the nature of the earth, it is they that the fairies and gnomes patterned themselves after when they decided to become less physical, and more non-physical, and to become more ONE with the energy play of the earth and the devas. Devas have been called nature spirits, sprites and sylphs for many years.

Overlighting angels are a bit more removed. They watch. They help channel energy to the areas they watch. They speak with the devas and feel empathy for all living creatures in their area but they do not intervene on a physical level as much as the fairies or the devas. They will and do help the devas and the humans clear negative energy from areas when they are called in, and they do help connect humanity to Source. But they do not shift the winds or the rains or the sun or make the plants grow swifter or taller. That is the work and the play of the devas and the fairies. Every piece of earth has an overlighting angel. Some watch small areas of earth, and some watch very large pieces of earth. Most pieces of earth have several overlighting angels watching over them, at different levels, feeling different levels of connection and inter-personal connectedness. So, as your home or street has an overlighting angel, so does your city, and the general area of your state, and the area of your country, and also your entire country. Your entire planet has an overlighting angel called the Sun, and also the Moon.

Many fairies work with the devas and are ONE with devas but they are not always the same thing. In the beginning the fairies and gnomes were creatures just like you and the animals. No different. But they chose to become less physical than your physical and more than our non-physical. They had interacted with the orbs and devas and decided that they wanted to incarnate as beings closer to that. So they are on a very high vibration, almost impossible to see, like the orbs, for most humans. But they ARE there. Nothing you do can harm them, for they exist next to you, but not with you. They play with the elements and the orbs but are physical enough that they can enjoy the physical aspects of your reality as much as they wish and choose. Thus the stories of their very long life spans, for time takes very little toll on their light-bodies.

ELVES

Can you tell me some information about elves? How are they different from fairies?

Elves are not different from fairies. They are part of the fae community. What many think of as fairies, small twinkly lights and beings, elves are not like that. They are like fairies in that they are multi-dimensional and able to shift in and out of your reality. They can be large or small, though generally they are human like in shape and size. They are more serious. Less dramatic. More protective of the wild lands. Less involved with people. They feel and act more removed from humanity's current world. If the elf blood runs within your family line, you will still connect with them and your souls return to that dimension when you sleep and between your human lives. One's elf side is what draws some to the land, and can help people see the truth of all things.

SUMMER TIME

Summer is the fruited time of the year, in your half of the planet, and the animals and plants are singing in joy. Why do you humans not join them? Why do you not also raise up your voices and your hearts and sing?

The answer is simple: you have removed yourself so much from this aspect of living, that you no longer see it. You go to your large supermarkets and stores, and you do not know where things come from, or when. The availability of produce and product is a wonderful abundant lesson for humanity, but it also has its darker side: you have forgotten what joy there is the abundance of nature and of the fruitful times, and so you do not know anymore what the feeling is that you are trying so hard to recreate on a daily basis. You came far from the fields to the cities and markets so that you would always feel this fruitful feeling, and now you have lost it. In order for humanity to reach its next level of evolution, this feeling must be regained. You must remember what this feeling is. Pick strawberries. Wander in fields and in parks. Watch the birds rejoicing. Connect with your greater selves, with your souls, and ask them to help you recreate this feeling. Ask the devas and overlighting angels of your areas to send you all the fruitful lessons of joy and grace that they can, and to help you lift your spirits. Be well. Be in Joy.

BUTTERFLIES

Butterflies are always a good sign, YES! You are evolving, and everyone else is, too - during this time, be like the butterflies. The best part about them is that they don't have to think about this process – the go into their cocoon and literally melt, even their brain, and then they come together again with the same soul, the same brain, in a majorly evolved body. It just happens. This is the beauty of allowing. The butterfly doesn't think about it. It doesn't feel bad about being able to fly when some of her friends cannot yet. It doesn't feel guilt or wonder if it's really the right time. It just knows. It just does. It allows the process, and everything goes as it should. Because of this act of allowing, plants around it flourish and are pollinated, and beauty reigns everywhere it goes.

LAWN TREATMENTS

Do not treat your lawn with pesticides, or even diatomaceous earth: the beneficial insects will not thank you. Instead, smudge your yard, and keep it trim. Call in the devas to help you.

THE AURORA BOREALIS

The Aurora Borealis is a diminutive form of a supernova, of the consciousness-raising light, of the god-form direct that inhabits you all. It is there to remind you humans, always, that you have come from the light and are of the light and that you can create such miracles and beauty such as the play of lights on the snow, both in physical though-form creation and in your hearts.

We want you all to know that the world you live in is a paradise, filled with all the joy and love and laughter you need if you will but allow it to fill your life and being. You are loved, you are whole, and there is nothing outside of yourself that can change that.

Feel the love you felt when you chose your body to incarnate. Feel the joy you felt when you were ready to be born. This is a time of creation and miracles, a time for gods to walk the earth, co-creators every one of you. There is not another way to be, just a way to not BE. Love yourself, and you will feel the light.

There is much, so much, for you to do on your planet: go do it! Create! Laugh, live, cry and be at peace. Love love love. There is nothing else for you to do but give and receive love and feel at one with your true self.

CROP CIRCLES

Crop circles originate from various locations and energies. Some are initiated by nature devas or spirits, some come from our "alien" parent worlds such as Sirius and the Pleiades, and some come from deep within mass human consciousness. They all act with one purpose. Crop circles activate the energies in a particular place to align with the energies of the message. Crop circles are not composed of letters or even direct symbols that can be categorized like an alphabet, rather they are direct manifestations of a particular thought form or message. The locations where they are drawn are chosen for various reasons: some originate there so because it is that locale that most needs that particular energy which the circle carries. Some places area chosen because it is know that the circle will be found and circulated in the best fashion. Sometimes humans make the circles and they are deemed fakes. But what it is not understood is that even if the humans making the circle believe they are making up something for fun or a joke, they are actually producing a true and valuable message produced for the beneficial evolution of mankind, directed by mass consciousness for the highest good. There are NO fake crop circles. All are of value. The best way to work with crop circles is to gaze at them. Even a quick perusal of the images will harness their energies and shift your cells to align with the higher message. A longer gazing meditation upon the circle will do even more. The sharing of crop circles in communities is a valuable act for humanity. Slide presentations with soothing music are nice, as are YouTube messages and movies. A video designed and marketed to the meditation market consisting of crop circles interspersed with naturally occurring Fibonacci spiral sequences would be very beneficial for everyone, and well received.

Crop circles are the key to the universe, but you have yet to find the doorway. Your people on your planet still live in fear and pain, and are not ready to use the circle yet. But still we, the souls not with you, come back and paint them in your fields and lands for words and symbols are power, and as the symbols are shared the people rise in power. You cannot translate the symbols for you have not the true words which are rooted in joy and love. But you can and should study them in a relaxed state, and enjoy their powers.

Crop circles are not a threat, or a warning or anything to fear, but something we share with you because you asked us to help you remember what you knew before you were born there in your physical reality. These messages are keys to your forgotten past, your heritage, your birthright. Slowly, they help you become that which you have wanted to be.

LEY LINES

How can we heal areas of land that have damaged energy, such as "black streams", weakened ley lines, or places subject to geopathic stress?

Drum there. Once a week for three weeks, on each spot, with much intention. Drum the vibrations back into the earth, call the earth devas to help you heal those spots. It is very easy, just a few minutes of drumming on each spot for three weeks. This can be done anywhere, with drums. Rattles and Rainsticks will not work. Only drums, didgeridoos, singing bowls, flutes or bells. It lasts a long time and is more in tune with the land of "western" nations than the earth acupuncture, as those methods are more in tune with China and the Philippines. In Japan they do much with their ancestors and guardian spirits to heal such stress lines. That too can work here, though for many we feel the drum is the best choice.

MANDALAS

Mandalas are a way to access spirit. Much like Celtic knot work or labyrinths, they help lead the mind out of ordinary reality and into the sight of spirit.

EARTH CHANGES

The planet went through a major shift in 2008. The older you were, the harder it was for your physical body to become accustomed to this change. The earth is not wobbling more or less, or spinning at a different rate, but its energetic, magnetic essence shifted to a higher rate of vibration which effected your equilibrium. Quickly, most bodies were able to adjust itself. Children shifted very quickly. Your bodies had to calibrate itself to match the planet's new vibration.

The effect of this new calibration will not be immediately apparent, but it will bring a higher rate of health and well-being on the planet. People will need less food. People will use calories more efficiently, whether they are under- or over-eating. This shift was planned to occur later, but was implemented earlier to facilitate an easier ascension for the masses that were facing starvation at the time. It is also affecting the animals and plants, and all will be more efficient now, which will benefit both the beings and the planet's climate and ecosystems.

The earth is waking up, waking up, and she is calling out to all her peoples: wake up! Wake up! Wake up! There will be quakes and shakes and events in every major region, so that everyone may hear her calls. These are simple reminders to be more alert, and to participate more consciously in life. LIVE your life. Do not let it roll by without jumping in with both feet. Don't get to the end of your physical incarnation and realize that you missed it. Yes, you can always begin again, and start a new life, but why not live your life right NOW, right where you ARE?

There are, of course, a lot of you who do not want to participate, who do not want to wake up. When directly presented with the question, "do you wish to stay here on Earth?" some of you will answer: ""No! Get me out of here!" And so those people will be "checking out." Still more of you want to start fresh, and grow up completely in the New Age rather than in the older body and mind which you have. Those, too, will be checking out. Your bodies are temporary, and your stay is voluntary. Return anytime, leave anytime that is the agreement.

ASCENSION SYMPTOMS

I am dizzy, what is going on? I have heat in my head and I hear ringing sometimes in my ears.

The dizziness is from earth shifts – you are shifting with the earth, fast, rapidly, moving and spinning and you are evolving and you can feel it. You are getting new chakras, all new, faster spinning ones.

Whhhhheeeeeeeeeeeeeee!

The heat in your head, silly one, you know it was your fears melting away. Can't you feel it? You try to think your fear thoughts and they don't stick anymore. They are not valid, and they are gone. POOF.

You are shifting, just as the earth is shifting. As your body adjusts to the new energies, you will have what are called ascension symptoms. Be easy, and they will pass with grace.

GLOBAL WARMING

My heart is sad to think about how global warming is changing the ocean temperatures and the food chain for its aquatic life, and how it is affecting the ice caps and the animals that live on the ice. And as I see development, I am always saddened to think of the loss of habitat for wildlife. Can you help me to see these changes more clearly?

You humans are so reactive, we enjoy watching you sometimes. It is very silly, and yet also sad to see that you forget so easily what you know in your soul-heart. Extinction is impossible. All exists for all time. You may not see it or feel it, but it is there. Just as every word you utter goes on for all time, so do the thought-forms and feelings of the animals, and so do ALL souls. Do you think that these animals are leaving without a choice? Do you think that they did not help create the world we live in? Again you humans give yourselves more power than the other beings on your planet. The earth is ascending. It is improving. Some species are choosing to end their time on earth because the experience which they offer is no longer to be relevant on your sphere. Some species are choosing to move to another earth which is similar, but farther behind in its

64

evolution, so that they can help there. Some species are moving ahead and holding the space on the new earth for the rest of you. And some species are simply choosing to move on to other experiences. All life is wild. All life is equal. You humans are tearing down plants and trees to be in your current experience, but new experiences which you cannot imagine will blossom out of the manure you create from the dead.

The climate you have on the planet is not the best climate you can have, merely the one you are most used to. The heat will level out, and more of the world will be like the tropics that your people flock to on their vacations. This is why: the planet is accommodating your desires for a leisurely planet. The hardships of the north, of the arctics, is not vibrationally compatible with the ease which you seek on your planet. The designation of the warming as a crisis is inaccurate, but good in that it spurs on your people to seek better ways of using and creating energy. Soon free energy will exist within your reality, as it does in ours.

WATER

Water is a major theme right now for so many people. It is a vital element on your planet, but one that so many ignore. The water elementals on Earth have been angry for a very long time about how man has mistreated them. There are many parables throughout the world of the ungratefulness of mankind for the bounty of the sea, of lakes and rivers. Yet the water elementals have some of the greatest lessons to teach man, if only he will listen.

To begin, the water elementals want you to remain clear and open. They want you to sing more. They want you to spend more time with your arms wide open, ready to receive.

DOLPHINS

On all levels, dolphins connect with the etheric body first, then the mental, the emotional, and the physical. They feel their way into a person. This is why they affect people so deeply, without most people understanding it, because they actually create an etheric link, much like a modern wireless data link, where they download all your information, and your blueprint, into their own, investigate it, and connecting. Often, being near a dolphin, even through glass, is a healing experience because they will actually reprogram areas that they can see need to be fine-tuned in the etheric blueprint. It is something that is second nature to them, much like if you saw a glass on the edge of a table you would reach out without thought and push it back a couple inches, or straighten a crooked painting on wall as you walk by.

WINTER & SNOW

One of the greatest things you can do for yourself in winter is to take leisurely walks outdoors. Your physical self is re-energized by the beauty and cleansing energy of nature, and thus is more able to fulfill the desires of your greater spiritual purpose and being when you return from these walks.

As you move into cold seasons, people are inside much more, and that is also good. There is time to go within yourself, and be more to yourself. Winter is a good time for introspection and meditation. Sometimes you find it difficult to stay still, and winter is a time when you mourn your disconnection from nature. Do not worry, for nature always returns. Mother Earth misses the days when all humans rejoiced in her snows and storms. For they are a time a cleansing and renewal, a time to enjoy. When it snows, remember to be as a child, and delight in the snow. Fall into a snow bank. Make a snowball. Get wet, get cold. And then go inside and sit by the fire and just be. Drink hot cocoa and eat warm soup. Take nothing for granted, for all is a manifestation of your wonderful ability to create, and you always create what is beautiful. Rejoice in your surroundings.

For you humans, snow storms have taken on different meaning than they used to hold. Now, when your lives are so busy, they are a gift to make you stop, motionless, forcing a retreat from the hurry and stress that you are in the midst of. Only the most stubborn of you refuse to listen to the snow, refuse to stop and relax for those few gifted hours. For the animals, and for humans past, snow is also a time to rest, but not because they are stressed or too busy. They welcome the rest, it is not forced upon them or resented in any way. As with your children who live for snow days and sledding, so too do the animals enjoy the peacefulness of the snow and the joy it brings. For the Earth the snow is a tool. She brings on this period of rest to ensure that all are ready for the following period of un-rest, of activity, of hustle and bustle and clamoring. This is not the clamoring of economy or war, but the activity of evolution, of change, of shifts. Every snow heralds a quiet shift in vibration, a time of consciousness about to rise. The rest, the peacefulness of the spirit, allows the physical bodies of the beings which inhabit the earth to better accept the higher vibration. As the earth shifts to her highest vibration, there will someday be less snow. People will seek it out for its restorative qualities. But that is neither here nor now. It IS there. Then. Do not seek the future, it will come soon enough.

Live in the present. Relax in your snow. Be ready to ascend another step higher.

LUNAR ECLIPSES

Lunar eclipses are messages to man that it is the right time to begin anew, to refresh old ideas, to solidify plans. They are, in effect, New Moons backed by the full growth potential of Full Moons. Voids, clean slates, starting and ending points. Focus on the starting, not the ending, for the ending comes of its own accord when you no longer focus on it. Focus on what you want, what you really really want, when, and how. Imagine all the details. Be specific.

CHEMTRAILS

Ah yes, the trails in the sky. They are not anything major to worry about, we say. Your government is trying to slow global warming and also sometimes it sprays them to help cover up parts of the earth so satellites from other countries cannot see what it is doing. There are many secret operations. They are all very silly. There is nothing in these chemtrails that will hurt you or your children. They are not inoculating you.

You should also know that global warming does not pose a real problem to most of your people and species on the planet. Any species leaving the planet at this time is moving on to another planet for their continued evolution. All will be well

POISON IVY

A long time ago, poison ivy was considered a power plant. It was used by people throughout the Americas much like tobacco, smoked for hallucinations and healing ceremonies. As it gave the power to see the future, it was used wrongly, and because of it many battles were won and many died, and so the poison ivy transmuted itself to give rashes, so that it could no longer be used. It cannot be smoked, or taken internally, in any form other than homeopathically. The more you have killed in your past lives, the more sensitive you are likely to be to poison ivy. Those who never killed are totally immune to it. It is not a punishment, but rather a booby trap. The more the wars of America rage, the more the ivy grows, and grows. Humans are encouraging its growth in preparation, to remind themselves in the future to kill less, and not at all.

HOUSE PLANTS

Some people seem to have an ability to have wonderful plants in their homes, but my plants always look rather poorly? Is it simply a matter of them using better soil, more nutrients, just the right amount of soil, proper pruning, regular dividing and replanting, etc.? Or is it that some people have an attitude toward the plants that really makes a difference?

Did you buy the plants with joyful anticipation or with deliberate thought? Or, were these plants thrust upon you by the goodwill of others or on someone else's advice? Did you carefully look between plants of the same species to see the one that created a smile in your heart? If you and the plants are not a good energetic match, they will leave you in the only way they can: by dying and returning in another seed somewhere else, to someone else. Light and water matter, of course they do, just as you need sleep and food, but if the plants were joyous they would survive even poor conditions.

GARDEN PESTS

What may I, can I, and should I do to prevent the animals (woodchucks, deer, rabbits, chipmunks, squirrels, and birds) from eating all of my crops? I usually have nothing left over.

There are several steps to clear this issue from your reality. First, when you plan your garden plot, sit quietly in the center of the area and clear your mind. Call in the surrounding energies of the property: the nature spirits such as devas and fairies, the earth herself, the animals, the elements. Let them know that you are searching for a layout and plan of action that will bring the most harmony between the land, all local beings, and yourself. Ask them if there are specific areas that should lie dormant that year, where different crops should go, and if there is anything in particular anyone wants planted, and where and how. Ask if there are amendments which need to be made to the soil or the layout. Let your mind remain open to the possibilities and new ideas: some things may seem outlandish or obvious, some ideas you may not get around to incorporating, while others you may embrace whole heartedly: the important thing is to begin the communication process. Make sketches and plans and sit with them for a while. If something strikes you as undesirable, go back to your garden and re-open the lines of communication. See what comes to you.

When you are communicating with the hungry animals in particular, ask them if there are particular crops you could plant just for them, or perhaps if there is a small share of your crops they would accept if you left them in a particular place (or places) for them as an offering or tithe. You will most likely find that they want, in reality, very little from you, and have just been waiting for you to make the gesture.

Sometimes, you may find resistance from one of the animal kingdoms. One type of animal may not be interested in your offers, or may say they are but then go ahead and eat their fill anyways. Do not be disappointed. This is a new process for you, and may need to be done more than once until you get the hang of it. The gardeners at Findhorn who employ similar practices took many years of communication to benefit in some areas of the farm, while other aspects came easily. Simply relax with it. Trust yourself. Enjoy yourself. Remember that there is *no lack* in your reality. There is nothing that you cannot have, be, or create. All is at your fingertips, and all is well: expect the best.

THE DIVINE FEMININE & MASCULINE

You are surrounded by emissaries from the Divine Feminine. You live on a planet that is intrinsically divine and feminine. When you open to one feminine energetic, you will open to them all. So, how do you connect to the divine feminine? Not through action. Not through trying. Not through ordering it to be there for you or by requesting its presence. To connect to the divine feminine is to *receive*. RECEIVE. Because it is already there. You are ALREADY connected to it. If you were not, you would be dead. Literally. Physically dead. You cannot live on earth and not be connected to the divine feminine. You can, however, not *hear* or see or breathe or know the divine feminine. Yet, you have been born into a time of great distortion for the paradigms of masculine and feminine energy, and a time of great healing. It is important, as a healer, to embody these aspects of Source in their most divine forms. The question is, how?

The masculine is the solar, supportive aspect of source. It is the part that nurtures and fuels creation, the energy that drives will. It is best embodied by love and honor.

The feminine is the lunar, creative aspect of source. Ever changing, ever making. It the passionate seed of evolution, the will to expand and manifest.

We know these aspects well in their distortions, where the feminine is receptive and meek, and the male is domineering, angry and controlling. The distortion is the root of much conflict both in personal relationships and the world, and it is our job as shamans to repair it. The male needs to be uplifted by the beauty and passion of the female. When the female does not follow her beauty and passion, then the male becomes uninspired and falls into old, heavy distortions of male patterning. The feminine becomes secondary to the male, when in fact it is the masculine role to support the female as she uplifts the family and the human race at large.

Part of the healing process is to nurture the male and allow its return to its true center of love, protection, and honor. This is no easy task because the distortion of the divine masculine has also distorted the feminine, but it is possible. A simple exercise is to honor the male and female aspects of yourself truthfully and fully with positive affirmations.

Another way to balance your masculine and feminine selves is to work with the six-pointed star, or its 3D manifestation, the merkaba.

THE MERKABA

A six-pointed star consists of two triangles, one pointing down (the feminine) and one pointing up (the masculine.) You can use the symbology of a six-pointed star to harness male/female balance, as well as the paradigm of "As Above, So Below." The masculine triangle draws down energy from source, and grounds it in the physical. The feminine triangle draws energy up from the Earth and expands it into material being-ness. When you work with the star as a 3-D object, each triangle becomes a 4-sided pyramid, or tetrahedron. On their own, in scared geometry the tetrahedron represents the energy of fire, and indeed, the merkaba is an active, living matrix that can be used for creation. It is referenced in ancient Kabbalah texts as a fiery wheel, a vehicle allowing prophets and angels to travel the heavens.

Every human has a merkaba that surrounds them on the astral plane (not be confused with your aura). This merkaba, when it is working properly, can be used to travel astrally, to increase your energetic connection to the physical realm, and to travel to other dimensions. Unfortunately, with the distortion of the masculine and feminine aspects of self which we discussed earlier, most people's merkabas are not working as they should be. Indeed, for many people, they are not working at all.

So, how do we fix it? You make sure that it is fully loaded, shining and spinning.

When running properly, a merkaba is a vortex of manifestation, an energetic computational machine which interacts directly with source to create the reality you are wanting. If you haven't consciously programmed it, it's not creating much of anything. Your merkaba is your creative matrix that allows you to combine your soul intention with the spark of god-energy and literally create your reality however you want. Like a crystal, it can be programmed through meditation and by setting your intention. All that is required is for your merkaba to be actively spinning, which is done through breathing exercises and habit. Daily, spend 3-10 minutes spinning your merkaba. The way this is done is to breathe deeply and visualize that you are rotating the feminine, down-pointing tetrahedron clockwise (creating a high-pressure vortex that draw energy upwards for creation) and rotate the masculine, up-pointing tetrahedron counter-clockwise (creating a low-pressure vortex that draws energy "down" for from Source.

With enough practice, your merkaba will be reprogrammed and spin regularly without maintenance. Besides helping energize your physical body and increase your connection to source, this is useful, because your merkaba is an amazing tool for personal manifestation and creation. When it is spinning, all you have to do is instruct it as to what you would like it to create. If there is negative energy in a room emanating from a person or geopathic stress, you might program your merkaba to deflect it. If you are wanting a specific job, your merkaba can reach into the energy matrix of the Earth and help conspire to create this specific reality. Or, you can give overarching instructions such as "I program my merkaba to flow with ease in this physical earth reality and to see that all my needs and desires are fulfilled for the highest good of all involved." You are the only one on earth who can work with or program your merkaba. No other human or healer may influence the programming of your merkaba, although a healer may work on your breathwork and energy patterning to help facilitate merkaba activation.

Another thing you can do to help heal the world is spin your merkaba and imagine yourself as a fractal, expanding that energy out into the world, realigning the masculine feminine as it ever-expands. Fractals are, at their core, the repetition of one energy as it swirls every outward, repeating itself over and over in perfect resonance. In this way, you are, we are, all IS, perfect fractals of source. We all hold source within and recreate it perfectly, exactly, in every wave and sine, in every atom, again and again.

KUNDALINI
AWAKENING

The earth is in ecstasy. She is full in the creation of her new self, and reeling with joy. Soon, the birthing will begin. Have you heard the Earth Mother groaning as she begins her labors? Have you felt the ground shaking even when the scientists say it is not? She is beginning her birthing, a birthing which will raise all beings on Earth to new heights of consciousness. Be peaceful and still, be good babies, and relax. Position yourselves peacefully at the opening of the canal, and be ready for slow, gentle easing into your new world. These labors are only beginning, and will take years. But the early signs are there. She has begun.

As the earth realigns, your root chakras must also realign in order to receive energy from the earth properly. This is most often experienced as spasms or twinges in the pelvic region of the body. The earth provides the energy which runs up and down your spine, your kundalini, and if you cannot receive the energy, then you will have no kundalini.

But this is not just about energy, this is also a physical evolution, of the earth and of the people. Everyone is having these spasms in their sexual organs from time to time, though of course most do not talk about it. Anyone who does not have them at all over the following decades will not survive long on this planet, for they will be as if without food, starved, and die.

VORTEX TRAVEL

To travel the vortexes you must first fix them in place. Any vortex that is fixed in place, and which you have experienced and become one with, you may travel to and from. If you do not do this, you may become lost in the in between, or come out in a place different than you intend. This is good work. We would caution you not to travel to places outside of the planet for many years, until you have mastered the vortexes here and have met many times with the outdwellers. There are infinite out-places to land, and few where your body or mind would survive. First, you must meet the outdwellers, and once they have taught you where to go and how to travel then you can began to leave the planet.

Meanwhile, we would caution you to also make sure that you finishes your work here your family and your life. Becoming a **traveler** is an energizing choice, but it is also an easy means to run away from your life, the life you chose to work with. The more you **travels** the less **present** you will be, and there may be consequences.

MANIFESTING MONEY

You were taught that money is something you all have to work hard, every day for. You have tried to fight against this teaching, for you know it is not true, and yet the belief has persisted within you. Your family and teachers are so strongly connected to you that still many of their beliefs are your beliefs, though you would wish and believe it were not so. Many of your hard times in life have stemmed from this connection, for their beliefs, and thus yours, are at odds with your high vibration and the KNOWLEDGE that it holds. In order to release this connection, you need to understand that you can be with you family, and your culture, yet not at one with it. In your heart, you have felt an outsider, and have not understood that everyone feels the same way, regardless of the degree of their differing beliefs. Everyone disagrees, and on your planet, your people have been taught that to disagree if to be at odds with those around you. We DISAGREE. Your greater self DISAGREES.

To disagree is to be true to your self, to allow everyone to be true to themselves, to allow every being on planet a creative reality that is theirs alone, and true to their own beliefs and desires alone. This is a beautiful reality to choose, and if you believe that others are allowing and accepting your difference of opinion, it will be so.

You also need to let go of the concepts of "starving artist", "wounded healer," and other similar archetypes. Immerse yourself in the lives of the well-fed artists. Become one with their realities. This will help you accept your own feeding and prosperity. Rent movies, go to library.

Whenever you have received prosperity, many of you have also felt guilt about your luck and your success. This guilt has turned the tide of prosperity away from you even as your joy and power of manifestation have attracted it to you. Good affirmations for you would be that "I am a money magnet and I deserve all the wealth and success that come to me. I am unique, and I am a wondrous being, and the world is in need of my beliefs and my art to be complete. There is only pride in the things which I create and attract, and every day I am accompanied by joy and laughter."

THE SELF

There is nothing outside of yourself. Everything you think you know, everything you think you know, see, smell, touch, feel – it's all in you. It all is you. You are not the only creator of your universe, you are not alone. How can you be alone when you are all together, when every being, every cell, every *thing* in the universe is **inside** YOU? It's all in there. Your atoms, your cells, your makeup is ever so much more complicated and more vast than your science has even begun to discover. Inside you, is the Milky Way. Inside YOU, is god. Inside YOU, is ALL. And inside her, and inside him, and inside that, and inside this. Everything contains the entire universe inside of itself. Not just the possibilities of the universe, but the entire vastness of ALL that IS.

You think you know, but you don't.

You think you comprehend, but you can't even begin.

And that is OK. Because that in part of ALL, too. This is meant to be. It's all inside you, and you are perfect in your condition, in your comprehension, and in your becoming. You are growing just as you should be. There is nothing that is missing or should be better or should be different. It is all perfection, as are you.

Do not worry. Do not fret. Do not think you must give up anything, or fear anything, or do anything differently. Just be. Just be you. Give yourself up to the wonder of the unfolding that is the perfectly you, you now.

You are blessed and you are loved for you are the creator of ALL that is, of the LOVE that is, you are the IT and the WONDER and the JOY and the NOW. Fractals are, at their core, the repetition of one energy as it swirls every outward, repeating itself over and over in perfect resonance. In this way, you are, we are, all IS, perfect fractals of source. We all hold source within and recreate it perfectly, exactly, in every wave and sine, in every atom, again and again. You are one of many. Many lightworkers, many radiant beings. You are all, all radiant beings. All on earth. Even the most lowly, even the most "unholy", is a radiant being. You are all equal creators of wonder and amazement. That is, you amaze us every day, every moment. You are all crucial energetic wheels in the workings of the universe. Without you all, there could be no time, no creation, no real new wonder in the world. Without you, there would be no-thing. You make it all. You have raised the energies of the universe to a place so fantastic, so holy, so high and light-filled, that you are pushing the limits of the universe further and further every moment. Everything you do, everywhere you go, you are contributing to the growth of us all in ways that you cannot even begin to imagine.

And so we love you. And as we are all part of your experience, connected to you as all the energy in all of creation is connected and yet not currently participating in your physical world, we are filled with wonder at everything you do. We rejoice in your every moment the way a parent rejoices in every step of its newly walking child. We clap when you clap, we sing when you sing. When you cry, we sing for you still, for we know you are so much more than what you fear and what you mourn. We know that you are with us, still, and that you are beings of such light and such power that if you would but open your eyes even half-way to the truth of your power, you would release all your fears in that instant.

So that is what we would like you to do. We want you to open your eyes. We want you to see with your third eye, with your dreaming eyes, with your physical eyes, and with the eyes of your soul. We want you to SEE. To BE what you are, to SEE it and believe it. Than BE ALIVE with it.

That's all we want. It's not so hard, really, we promise. Intend it to be so, tell your eyes to be open, and then do not discount what you see.

Believe what your heart sees, for sometimes it sees more truth than your eyes. And vice versa. You **know** what is true, and what is not. You know who you are, and who you are not.

Open your eyes to the truth of your being, and the reality of your life, and you will see that you are gold, that you are magic, that you are filled with the power and the glory and the light and the love of ALL that IS.

REINCARNATION

What can you tell us about reincarnation? Why do some religions and tribal cultures have reincarnation as core belief, while others believe there is only this one life?

Reincarnation is real, but not everyone comes back to this planet. So for some, there really is just this one life on your planet. Some leaders have found it beneficial to spread the idea that there is only one life because that helps people focus all their intent on this life, and be more ferocious in pursuing their dreams. Others have decided their tribes would be happier without the guilt and regret that can come from a bad decision that may ruin this one lifetime, and that when one know you are coming back again, there will be time to redeem oneself. Single actions become less important than holistic evolution. It does not matter what one believes, for there are only two goals for souls incarnating on earth: to help the earth and her beings evolve, and to practice the art of creation and physical manifestation. There are endless ways to partake in these goals, and almost all beings on earth are doing so with great success.

If you confirm the concept of reincarnation, is there any sequence, system, or criteria for whether one comes in as a person, animal, fish, insect, reptile, etc.? And would plants also be part of this concept of reincarnation?

Yes, yes, yes, any that is energy can hold the spark of a soul within. You can live within a rock for a time if you wish. Your soul energy can be anywhere in the universe that it desires. It is often in several places at once, and certainly it is never all here on earth. There are many systems for reincarnation, and some criteria, but they are self-imposed by souls. Some souls enjoy following rigid paths of ascent, or staying with classes of species on planets. Others bounce throughout the universe with little planning.

Animals and humans are the same. They are not different soul groups, they all come from the same place, and yes they can cross over between species. They often do not, but this is because the souls are particularly attuned to particular species vibrations.

To come to Earth, souls have to be accepted into mass consciousness by the sun, who is the overlighting angel of your system. If one does not have the desire to work on earthbound evolution or creative physical manifestation, then one does come to earth. There are other places where one does not have to apply. This is simply one "school" of thought, here where you live.

SOUL NAMES

Souls do not have actual "sound" names as you perceive them – rather, the best we can do is give you sounds best approximate the vibration that soul carries. Each soul carries a unique vibration, like a fingerprint or a snowflake. In fact, the reason every fingerprint is different is because it is manifesting the vibration of the soul's name. The whorls and swirls are created by the vibration of your soul, what you call a name but what is really only a sound, a manifestation of the vibration that resonates everywhere you go.

We communicate our name as Eden, not because of the word's meaning or representation, but because the collective vibration of our group energy is best approximated to the vibration of the sound, Eden.

ORBS & PHOTOGRAPHIC ANOMALIES

What are orbs? I have a couple of photos of unusually large orbs near the ground where my dogs have just chased after something, but nothing is physically there. Are the dogs seeing the orbs and chasing them, or are the large orbs the luminous bodies of animals that are in that area. Would that then mean that the smaller orbs might be the luminous bodies of other animals, such as birds, that are in the area? Perhaps luminous bodies floating out of the body in the sky above the birds?

The orbs you see are not nature spirits per se, or animals either. They are soul pieces sent to earth to watch over the planet and different physical activity. They are pieces of souls like us, and like you, which allow us to SEE what is going on in your physical reality. They are not wholly un-physical, which is why you can photograph them, but neither are they incarnated nor tangible. Some are higher or greater selves, some are guides, some are visitors. Some play with the winds and the plant kingdoms, and are what you would call your nature devas. They are all related to source. They are all ONE. You are all ONE. We are all ONE. We are all together all the time in all ways, you have but to see and hear it.

Orbs will come sometimes when called, and also if they feel the presence of joy, laughter, passion. Both Orbs and Fairies enjoy LIFE. Most fairies are filled with LOVE. Some are not, and play tricks and meddle too much. Hence the warnings in your fairy folklores. All orbs are filled with love. They are watching, observing and partaking. There are many ways of beings and orbs, just as there are many ways of being human.

Not everyone that is photographing the same scene obtains orbs in their photos. Is it possible that the orbs decide whether to reveal themselves, based on the person doing the photographing, or is it simply a technical difference between cameras?

It is not the orbs choice to reveal themselves, they are always there to see, but rather the viewer's level of vibration to SEE. Some do not wish to, or are not ready to, consciously or unconsciously. The photos capture what you are seeing inside, even what you do not KNOW you are SEEING.

On the orbs of different colors, does the color or size signify anything?

The color you see is not necessarily the color the spirit chooses, but how that choice is translated into your eye-color spectrum. Generally, the colors in your spectrum relate to the frequency on which the energy is traveling. They do not have particular meanings, just as the sizes are generally meaningless, much like the different sizes and colors of your own peoples: it is merely a random preference of the being at that time of incarnation. Overlighting Devas are more likely to show as larger orbs, and fairies and local nature spirits often show as small orbs, but they can be any size, and often are.

What is the "smoke" or "mist" that we see in so many orb photos?

The smoke in the photos is the ether, which is usually only visible on the ethereal plane, which the photographer was connecting with at those moments. Not an entity or a guide, but the plane that those beings materialize from. The smoke is a "seeing" beyond the orbs.

I photographed a strange rod of rainbow light moving through the trees. What is it?

Ah, you have photographed a traveler, a more rare occurrence as one never knows where they will be or for how long. Travelers are those beings which are not really visiting or observing, but just passing through this dimension very briefly on their way to other planets and places. They ride the light. The traveler probably did not even know you were there, but was just waiting in his appointed spot for the next ray of light to carry him on his way. This light is not sunlight, necessarily – it can be cosmic light from any direction, any spectrum. Often it is light which is invisible to you humans. That is why the image itself is so radiant and shimmers like a spectrum of colors, because to ride the light one has to become as the light.

What is the blue triangle of light I photographed?

The blue triangle is the merkaba people, the beings that have volunteered to help the deceased pass along to their next point of light. The light coming from their trees is their essence, and their energy. It is the way that the blue grid which you see is translated into photos. Moving, vibrating, so fast, it blurs. Some are non-incarnated beings, and some are lightworkers in an astral form working from the dreamtime.

LIGHTWORKERS

Are you a lightworker, an earth angel with a natural tendency to take on the pain or emotions of others? Most lightworkers work in some capacity or another to help transmute and process clearings for all of mass consciousness, and this can manifest as physical disease. It is important to recognize that this is what is happening, that this is a global phenomenon, and not to focus on the individual negativity or angst that you feel from one person or another. Begin to view negative people or situations simply as triggers or signposts from the universe. When one pops up, say to yourself, "Oh, here is something I need to clear." Shield yourself, and clear the energy. There are many, many ways to do this, but one of the simplest is bathing yourself in an orb of light of the color(s) of your choosing, pushing it out from yourself to create a buffer zone of comfort. Visualize the clearing, and then let it go, knowing you are protected.

SENSITIVITIES

Allergies and sensitivities pop up when we are sensitive to a situation, not the item itself. Sometimes, it is a past or parallel life trauma that is triggering our discomfort. Meditate on the situation and try to see the root of it. Seeing and knowing is understanding, and understanding brings release and clearing.

When one's soul consciously identifies a situation that is unpleasant, and one persists within it, the discomfort will only grow worse. It is one thing to remain in a situation that is not so great, but not fully realize, but once the soul *knows* that you *know,* both the body and the soul will feel somewhat betrayed by the mind/ego that is ignoring them and what it knows, and so they will work together to change your mind. Willingness to surround oneself with negativity at work and in life is another component to why one's body can have issues, basically attacking itself to get attention.

So, be gentle with your self. Take time to nurture yourself. Be compassionate with your self above all others: Only then can you truly be of service.

A MESSAGE FOR HEALING

Dearest beloved spirit. You are one with all of creation. All of creation loves you, and feels empathy for the state you are currently in. Love is pouring in to you from all sides, from above and below, from north east west and south. From deep inside you, your soul is sending you love, and from the farthest reaches of your galaxies, the arms of Spirit are reaching out to embrace you with love and expectation for a swift recovery. Open your heart and your mind to the love that surrounds you. There is nothing for you in the world of fear, in the world of sadness, in the world of depression. There is nothing for you in the words, thoughts, and deeds of negativity that will bring you comfort. Do not engage in acts of negativity. Reach for the light, in your heart and your mind. Reach for those people who would bring you comfort. Watch movies that make you laugh. Remember times when you have been happy, and imagine the things that would make you happiest right now. Allow yourself to feel these happy thoughts in the fullest sense, and soon, they will become your reality. You are a heartbeat away from recovery. You are one breath, one smile, away from pure love, and there is nothing that pure love cannot or will not heal. You are one with Spirit, and Spirit is one with you. You are much beloved. Be in love, and Be in Joy. Enjoy life! Be at peace, and be joy-FULL. All will be well.

THE BODY

Your body was happy to join you on your quest for physical immortality. It joined in this life with you to manifest that deliberately. However, not everything people do is directly congruent to that desire, and some things are actually in direct opposition to that desire. A body may become sad because it feels that you are not working WITH it, but against it, and in spite of it. Your body may feel that your spirit just orders it around, and does not ask IT what IT needs to do so. Even some of your detoxes and regimens are too taxing for the body, and can strip its sensitive LIGHTNESS from it: Your belief that what does not kill the body makes it stronger, is not always true or accurate. The body wants to be loved, and it is only through your love of it that it will have enough energy to regain the LIGHTNESS it had before you began abusing it, and it is only through a strong love and respect for the body that your body will agree to become immortal. Sometimes, what feels like emotional fear is not stemming from your soul, but rather from your physical body. Your body, your shell, on this planet has its own animating spirit that is not quite a soul but more like an elemental. It first had its spark of life when it came into this earthly reality in your first earth life. Since then, this elemental has accompanied you through all your earth lives, co-creating on the physical plane with you, as the caretaker of your physical body, so to speak. While your soul drives the bus, the caretaker looks after the bus. It tries to heal damage that is done to it, helps maintain cellular integrity. Perhaps most accurately, you could say that it is the blueprint for your body, with its own consciousness. If you see the blueprint as a sort of artificial intelligence – life and consciousness without soul, then that is what we are dealing with. So this intelligence, which we like to call your "body elemental", it has a lot of mistrust for the soul, and for this survival-based life on earth in general. It has felt pain so many times. Been abused and ignored and sidelined so many times. The relationship needs to be repaired. It needs to be reassured. That will help a lot with releasing the fear some feel. Stroke your arms, your legs, your torso as you would a cat and tell it: "I love you. You are cared for. Everything is going to be okay. You're safe now." When you are treating and nurturing yourself, don't forget to pamper your body, too – good food, good lotions, soft clothes, good sleep. You get the picture.

The main factor in attaining immortality is mind and spirit, the body is very happy to join the first two when they have progressed and raised their vibration high enough. It is happy to become crystalline. It is happy to live forever. It would like to return to the LIGHTNESS it once was, eons ago. It but needs a true partner, and not a director.

HEART-CENTEREDNESS

Humanity on your planet is entering a new era where actions and will begin in the heart, and humanity is entering Christ-consciousness. Christ-consciousness is not about the Bible, or Christ as most of you "know" him. It is about having a heart-centered consciousness. When a person enters Christ-consciousness, the center of the will is no longer in the solar plexus or the womb, as so many traditions have (correctly for their time) taught. The new center is the heart chakra, where all actions begin from a place of unconditional love.

The entire planet is entering this new form of mass consciousness. Many of your prophets and religious leaders had this form of consciousness, and now it has finally begun to filter into the mainstream mode of being. New chakras are being added to the human body to help this transition become permanent. When you are fully connected to Christ-consciousness, when unconditional love is the basis for all your actions, you are fully connected to Source Energy. Everything you do is for the greater good, and therefore also benefits you. Everything you feel comes from a place of love and joy, and therefore you will have a greater overall experience on Earth that is more firmly rooted in love and joy.

As with all change, this is not always easy. On a physical level, you may experience anxiety, palpitations, restlessness and fatigue. Your stomach may feel empty or vaguely upset as it loses its status as your chakra system's center. Daily chakra alignment exercises can help with these symptoms. Carrying stones like Danburite, Rose Quartz, Ruby and Hemamorphite can help. The flower essences Rose of Sharon and Coreopsis can help. Hawthorn Berry, the herb, is also good. Deep breathing exercises are beneficial, and any service-oriented activities will be helpful to bring the new consciousness into alignment with your soul.

Work on aligning your chakras with your new heart center, and everything else will fall into line. Those that you love, will show more love for you. Those that you fear will show more love for you. The news which darkens you nights will fade into the background. Life will become increasingly more positive. You will feel better. And all will be well.

NEW CHAKRAS, NEW BODY

Many of you have been feeling poorly in your bodies lately. Sick, sad, sore. You try to lift your thoughts to the sun, to joy and love, but you feel like you are being dragged down. Do not despair. Many of you have been receiving new chakra systems augmenting your previous 8 primary chakras. The timeline how and where you receive these chakras is different for everyone, but all are receiving an upgrade. While these additional chakras are aligning with your bodies, many of you are experiencing physical symptoms in line with a dead-cell throwoff: headaches, nausea, fever, soreness and more. To align with this new energy, drink more fluids, eat less, and take extra time to rest. When it is in place your new chakra system will automatically be harnessing more energy from source than previously. You will feel better, and joy and love will flow more easily. This new system was brought in by the desires of mass human consciousness to evolve. Rejoice, for your time is NOW!

What do I call these new chakras? What colors are they? How do I work with them?

The ones above your head are all the colors of the rainbow, like prisms. Below your feet they are earth and gold, going down. The new double ones acting holographically over the primary seven chakras are all pink, they are to harmonize the new body with love. The new one by your thymus is emerald green tinged with turquoise, and will help you speak with love, bring your love into your words and deeds. The ones in your legs are not new, they were there, but now you will work with them more. They are brick colored, and will help you draw energy always from the earth. They will help you connect further with the earth and with the devas. Must they have names? If they must, you can call the lower ones your **earth body** chakras, and the higher one your **soul harmony** chakras, for they are bringing in more of your soul into your body to harmonize with it better. The pink ones are transitional ascension chakras to your love body, as is the thymus chakra (which you can just call the thymus chakra). Your leg chakras act as your new taproots.

AURAS AND COLOR RAYS

Is there a connection between color of the aura of spirit and level of advancement?

No. Merely preference. Certain areas of spirit use color as a uniform, but they can also change their colors. It does not signify advancement, merely that they are choosing to be in the realm of that color at that time. There is far more freedom and far fewer rules in the realm of spirit than your humanity is capable of fathoming at this time.

EVOLUTION

You are at that point where humanity is receiving DNA upgrades, where you are ALL unlocking your full potential. It is your old world that is dying now, just as a new earth is emerging.

The biggest danger to your evolution at this moment is that too many of you will block your own progress. There is so much fear in your world that when wonderful new things appear you run and cower, scream and hide. Every small instance of change is automatically perceived and presumed a hindrance, a step backwards, when almost always it is a step forward.

50 percent of the children born in your planet's "developed" countries this year will grow to reach the age of 100. Do you really think this sort of evolution is happening without any accompanying improvements to the body itself? Of course, it is not. Just as your minds are expanding, just as your children are being born with a more intuitive ability to use and understand technology, so are their bodies being born with the ability to withstand all the changes of their environment and their world. As the world changes, so do the generations. So don't worry so

much. Don't fear so many events. Go with the flow. When you feel discomfort in your body, recognize that MOST of your pain and illness stems from your resistance to the changes in the core of your physical being. See if you can isolate your dis-ease, and then let it go. Recognize that you are shifting your very DNA and cellular makeup to create a new world. As the world changes, your physical body can and IS changing with it. You want to understand new technology? Your brain is rewiring itself at this very moment. You're afraid of chemicals in your food? Your digestive system has always had the ability to mitigate harmful substances and raise the vibrational quality of your food. This was a fully human ability and power of Christ, something that you all can do. **Intend** your food to be a healing, ascension building tool, and so it shall be.

Be ready for change. MAKE your own change. Get clear about what you would like to happen, because more and more as you shift into a higher vibrational Earth reality, what you want will occur with less resistance and at a faster pace. In essence, not only is time speeding up, but the delay between thought-creation and thought-manifestation is shortening. Watch what you think about – get rid of those doubtful, negative images in your head or all you shall sow in your life shall be weeds. Surround yourself with positive imagery and feelings to help your earth-gardens grow. Plant your seeds carefully, and use only the best imaginations and visualizations be your fertilizers.

The level of compassion and gratitude flowing in and around your species is growing. It is a beautiful thing to see and watch, for those of us who can see. More beautiful than any painting, more inspiring than any song of beauty. This is true divine inspiration, true connection to source, and it is growing every day on your planet. We are so pleased, so excited, to see your species growing by leaps and bounds.

There is a law among your scientists that the technology which limits computer processing will double in speed every 18-24 months. This law has been in place for over 50 years, and held true throughout this time. There has been a similar law about the vibration limiting your own processing speeds for eons. However, while the computer processing law is beginning to breakdown and processing speeds are now beginning to double more slowly, your own processing speeds are doubling and even tripling in record times. Your species is evolving by leaps and bounds, so fast you can barely even recognize the changes. But, we assure you, it is happening.

What's next? In the coming days and years each of you will face events in your lives that will force you to choose. Choose where to go, what to do, and who to be. Some of you will greet your changing lives with anxiety, others with joy. These changes are not going to stem from any sort of catastrophe, but rather from the culmination of your individual yearning. For many, there will be new jobs and new life plans. For others, there will simply be new daily routines, small changes in habit. But for all, we promise, there will be a significant shift and alteration in lifestyle and daily attitude. You'll be happier, and more fulfilled. The past will be the past, and you'll be fully rooted in the NOW.

EFT

The process of EFT, wherein one taps on meridians in the fingers or other points, appears to be a body-mind process for releasing points of resistance to positive manifestation and a means of staying focused on the release activity by being physically involved. Would Eden discuss the process and why and how it works? Does Eden have any guidance on how to improve upon the EFT process or how to better facilitate releasing resistance?

EFT involves tapping on meridian points, which are also chakra and mini chakra points. They are centers of energy on the body where emotions are likely to be stored. Tapping on them helps them "wake up" or activate, so that they can more easily release emotions or blockages. Further, when one is tapping and talking, the tapping allows one to remain more aware of how the body is reacting to the words that the mind is forcing it to say. So good body sensations are noticed. Bad sensations are noticed. This gets one in tune with the body as it is meant to be used: as a guide and friend that helps the mind stay in tune with the soul. When the mind is NOT in tune with the soul, or when your words are out of alignment with your desires, the you will feel physical comfort. Pay attention to it, and seek words and emotions that make you feel great in your body, then you will get to where you want to go quicker, easier.

MUDRAS & MEDITATION

The mudras, gestures made with the hands for meditative purposes, are sensational tools – meaning they actually bring the physical (sensation) in contact with the divine spiritual, and merge the two. They allow you to focus intent in a very good way. As we have said before, anything which focuses intentions is useful, and the more something has been used, the more people it has been used by, the more powerful it becomes. Thoughts have mass, and when you bring them together they coalesce into something more powerful than they were when they were just one single thought. This is why group prayer is so powerful. This is why mass hysteria is so damaging. This is why chants used over and over for many centuries carry so much raw potential. In the same way, mudras have been used for thousands of years, the symbols have become as homing beacons for universal energy. Merely make the gesture of desire, and immediately the desire is being fulfilled.

Must you use them every day? Surely the longer you hold a thought, the more often you hold an intent, the stronger Source's response will be. But if it does not bring you joy, do not do it. Meditate every day if you love it, if it is fun, if it challenges you in a way which makes your heart sing. When it becomes a chore, stop. And when you want to begin again, begin.

HOMEOPATHY &
FLOWER ESSENCES

Homeopathic remedies and flower essences both contain the vibrational essence of the original plant. Because they are diluted, they work primarily with the spirit of the remedy in tune with the spirit of the consumer, while medicinal tinctures work primarily with the physical aspect of the plant's constituents to attune the physical aspect of the consumer. Both have valid applications. Homeopathy works to shift one out of physical or emotional disharmony by harmonizing the spiritual cause. Herbal medicine works to shift physical disharmony by altering physical energy and *allowing* it to receive a better, higher vibration from spirit, thereby remedying the physical manifestation of distorted energy patterns. Homeopathic remedies are strengthened each time they are diluted because the practitioner *intends* it to be so. This powerful focusing of intent makes the remedy stronger. Also, the more the remedy is diluted the more it becomes anchored in vibration, rather than the physical, and the more effectively it can work on that plane.

SLEEP

How important is sleep if one reaches a high level of connection to source, positive thinking, and manifestation? I enjoy sleeping, but also enjoy staying up late to work or create? Is there a value in following a schedule of sleep and awake time?

Do not think that you are immune to the rules of earth-life. You need to sleep. You need to sleep every day. Your body would benefit from regular hours of sleep, and it is not healthy to sleep little during the week and play catch up on the weekends. Do not spend more energy when you are awake than you are replenishing during the night. This harms your physical body, which harms your spiritual and etheric bodies. When you do not sleep enough you are damaging your energy. If you want to be a powerhouse, you need a power SOURCE. You are like a rechargeable battery: your body also needs time to re-charge and download the energy it has received from food to enter into the other levels of your BEING.

Sleep. Eat. Do these things deliberately, and with intention. Do them as if they matter, because they do matter. They allow you to Be MATTER. And they allow you to MATERIALIZE. Creation takes energy, and to deliberately create, you must deliberately feed and recharge your creative vehicle: your body.

FEELING TIRED

How do you feel? Are you tired? Are you anxious? Do you jump from day to day alternately feeling relief and upliftment, only to be plunged back into emotionality and drama the following afternoon?

You are not alone. And it is OK. This, too, shall pass. As you know, and we know you know, there is a great awakening going on right now on your planet. But we also know you know that it is not always a pleasure being awoken and shifting gears to get out of bed. The alteration of consciousness is no task for the fearful. It takes courage and willpower to meet it head on with resilience and equanimity.

It is perfectly normal for your body and spirit to require time and rest to adjust to the current vibrational shift. Just as one gets tired after a long day of work or full day of activity, so might many of you feel very tired upon waking. Why? Because you are doing monumental work while you sleep, that is why! Your body's holographic imprint is shifting, while your soul is working hard on various levels.

Let's look at what your soul is doing while you First of all, while you sleep part of your soul is reconnecting with other souls in its soul group so that it can hold its highest vibration and receive energetic infusions that help you retain your highest resonance while you are awake. While you sleep you are connecting with source and realigning with your soul purpose. Then, your soul is working. Yes, working! Without exception, every soul has work that it does on the astral plane now and again. Some of you do this work relentlessly, night after night, and others of you do it sporadically, when you are called. Some of you help newer souls work align with the physical realm which is still so new and strange for them. Others of you work on the earth's gridwork, or healing physical functions in others, such as implementing new brain connections in sleeping bodies. Many of you who identify yourselves as lightworkers have volunteered yourselves to go into the afterlife dreams of souls who have passed on and help move them further out of the earth's atmosphere, where many, many souls remain still, lost in their dreams and addicted to the earth energies. This glut of souls in the outer realm of the earth's energetic layers is creating a vibrational drain on the entire earth's matrix: in order to shift fully and easily into a higher planetary vibration, the souls must be gently awoken and brought away from the earth, so that their energy stop creating interference and drag on the current situation. Basically, your air pollution on earth mirrors the soul pollution around you. As one situation improves energetically, so will the other, physically.

So do not despair that you are tired or feeling low. You are not shifting backwards, we assure you. You are simply experience growing pains. Continue to engage in activities which bring you comfort and support, whatever they may be. Wholesome food is good, blessing your food is even better. Meditating is good – anything which brings you inner joy and peace is helpful. Laugh. Be alive. Connect with the things that make you happy, and do less of what makes you unhappy. That simple. Yes.

EATING

Many people eat while standing, driving, walking, as part of their multi-tasking zoom-zoom behavior. Some say that blessing food before eating makes it vibrationally more valuable and supportive to the body. Others say that expressing gratitude for the food and visioning it as leading to a perfectly healthy body of perfect weight will eventually help the body to reach its optimum state. What does Eden advise as a practice or ritual of prayer before eating?

When you run around eating on the go in this manner, food is a hindrance to your flow of zooming. Food is not appreciated. Food is the enemy. Here, for you, this is why eating creates disharmony in your body. Blessing the food before you eat, sitting while you eat, these are merely tools: actions through which one may indicate **appreciation** for food. You can eat while you run: but you must appreciate the food. You must *bring the food into your vibration*. If you do not appreciate your food, you bar it from being vibrationally aligned with you, and when you bring it into your body, this creates spiritual and physical tension, which results in cellular mis-creation, which results in fat, diverticulitis, inflammation, indigestion, and a host of other possible physical signs of disharmony.

DRINKING WATER

It is accepted advice for good health, beautiful skin, weight control and release of toxins that we drink water. But, some people don't enjoy drinking water and drink coffee or tea, instead. Would Eden comment on what is really good for our bodies and why.

Water makes up over 80 percent of your body. It is what allows your body to function on an energetic level: water conducts the energy of Spirit through every cell of your body. Without water and minerals salts, your cells would not be able to connect with spirit. Distilled, or purified, water therefore is the least beneficial as it contains no minerals and cannot conduct energy. Coffee and teas are not recommended often because they contain constituents which alter your cells ability to harness and hold energy efficiently: they stimulate the cells to use all the energy of spirit in one big push, and then you are depleted. If you must flavor your water, use fresh juices which contain life energy and cellular sugars. The best thing for you is good quality fresh water: spring water or mineral water. Chlorinated water has other bad effects due to the fact that it affects the bacteria in your digestive areas. It does not matter if water has bubbles in it or not from an energetic standpoint.

RELEASING WEIGHT

Fear. Weight comes from being so afraid to be oneself and LET GO. The weight allows one to stay in place, to have excuses to stay still sometimes when one would rather not be more active in life. It is not laziness, but rather the fear of one's inability to not stop being active, and so people hold the weight in place. Were people to tell themselves to "be one with oneself, give in to their desires" they would soon know what they are to do. What they want, they desire, and what they desire will feel good. When they are feeling good, they are letting go and being in the flow of life. Then they will know what it is they are needing to do: whatever created that feeling of joy, do it again, and again, until the weight releases. If it does not feel good, do not do it. Learn to say no, instead of using tiredness as an excuse.

Also, for some, energetic or physical adjustments, such as visiting a chiropractor, need to be made. That will help the chakras flow better, and the chi, and thus the weight will normalize. Also some people need to rid themselves of their fears of being attractive, their belief that when they are at their most attractive they get into trouble. Then the weight becomes a protection for their

131

emotions. A physical wall to physicality. Use the intention "I am open, free and happy. I am safe without my shields. Love comes to me freely and flows from me freely and I feel love all around me."

For others, the weight is something that results from an inner sadness, fears within that have yet to release. These people should affirm: "I have all that I need to be happy, and I keep all that I need to be happy with me."

Excess weight is always stored by the body when it feels that there is reason to fear a lack of energy in the near future. Sometimes, excess weight remains because you have drained your power supply so drastically, on such a long-term regular basis, that your body tries to store extra power (for extra weight can be consumed when needed) in an effort to do what you have not. In that case, your body is trying very hard store energy for when you need it, since you have not taken care of it so many times before. So many bodies do not trust their spirit, as the soul has so often ignored or abused it.

On new parents, the weight appears because the body knows that there will be energy needed give off to the new child. In this era, when more fathers are helping energetically and emotionally with child-rearing, the fathers too are gaining weight during pregnancy.

Because fear in the body is a main cause of excess weight gain, one must first begin to lose the weight, and thus their fear, before optimum manifestation or well-being can occur: fear in the body is the problem. Not the weight.

ILLNESS

Physicians generally say that people do not get sick from temperature changes and weather changes, but only from infectious agents. However, people around the world regularly experience becoming ill after experiencing changes in temperature and weather, and even from changes in settings. Is there any value in trying to manage the physical conditions around one, or to being very careful to dress according to the weather? Or is our attitude about well-being the key determinant to whether we experience illness from physical changes?

Reactions to "infectious agents" and weather are all dependent on the state of your physical, energetic and etheric bodies. When you are in a perfect state of being, on all levels, you cannot get sick no matter what the infectious agent or setting is. If being cold makes you unhappy, it can also make you sick. If being hot makes you uncomfortable, it can also make you sick. If a strange hotel room is disturbing you mentally, you will also be disturbed physically. It is not so much your attitude about well-being, but your total *state* of well-being which determines how and when you experience dis-ease. If being dressed properly and being comfortable is important to your mental state, than you should definitely dress accordingly. If you are one of those beings who is comfortable in any state of physical being, then so much attention is not needed. One is not better than the other. It just is.

JOINT PAIN

Joints hurt because you harbor old pain. Pain is stored in the body, put away, to come out later when you felt you would be ready to deal with the pain. Later, your pain resurfaces. You must deal with old trauma, old pain, before the pain in your joints can be resolved. Resolve one, release one, resolve and release the other. Let go of your old sadness and guilt from the way your first family ended, and you will be able to feel your current joy fully. Remember that there is no reason in life to feel blame or anger, because all of life is just lessons and games, and we have all agreed to show each other way. Without having first felt sadness, you could not now feel its opposite. Without having first been abandoned, you could know true companionship. There are herbs that can help you with your pain (turmeric, cayenne, thyme, apple cider vinegar) but what will help you greater is for you to recall and release your old pains, so that your newer ones can stop their task of reminding you. Only you can release your self from your pain. To help you do so, look to flower essences of Roses and Jasmine, as well as the Alaskan essence from the sacred well. Remember, you are LOVED, and you are one with all. All are

one with you. We are ALL ONE, and we are all
LOVE.

CHRONIC PAIN

We want you to let go of your pain. We want you to forget that you have ever had chronic pain. We want you to forget that you ever had an injury. Forget all your old pains, and the new ones will lesson substantially. You may believe that because you have lived in pain, with pain for so long, that you have a high tolerance for pain, when in reality you have only had a high-capacity for *inviting in* pain. Lower your capacity for inviting pain. Lock the door to injury. Heal your energetic body on all levels, delve into your past lives and your future lives and your genetic line and release, release, release. Do a journey or meditation every day where you find something else to release, until everything has been cleared. If you cannot find the motivation to do it for yourself, know that every episode you clear is something you are clearing from your entire genetic line, for your children and your grandchildren, for your parents and your cousins. Know that every trauma you clear out will be cleared for you in future lives, and never need clearing again. Keep it up. Don't stop until you are truly done. This work will continue at least 30 days, maybe longer. For some of you, years. When it is finished, you will have no more pain, and your thoughts will also be clear. When it is finished, you will be relaxed as you have never been before. When you are finished, everything will have fallen into place and you will be well on your way to a brand new life filled with beauty, peace and love.

LYME DISEASE

This dis-ease began in the rats outside of the doctor's place, and is a karmic debt being repaid to humanity for experimenting on their bodies. The new generation are being born without karma, and so the disease is not for them what it is for you and the older generations. The older generations are hit the worst, with the bulk of the guilt being upon them. They knew they should not continue to mistreat animals the way they have, and yet they did not stop. Their guilt brought them this disease. It began with the affluent who had relinquished their liberal ideals in favor of gold and desires. It is not something sent from god or a retribution, but something invited in by humanity to burn off mass guilt. Many young children will manifest this illness now in a not serious form so that they will build a natural immunity to it for the rest of their life. They will not suffer after effects from this dis-ease, for they are at ease. Fear and expectation are two vehicles through which the disease travels. Young children, who are CONCIOUS may also CONSIOUSLY manifest the dis-ease in a mild form as they have been taught to do by the adults who discovered and utilized vaccinations. Like cures like, and the new generation is particularly well attuned with homeopathics.

TOXINS

Do we need to worry about the estrogenic compounds or other potential toxins in plastics?

You have surrounded your bodies with many items that are not healthy for your bodies. Someday, this will not be so. But you have always been surrounded by various unhealthy things, and slowly, you figure it out. When you discover something is not good for you, the logical thing to do is either to eliminate its vibration from your vicinity, or to *alter* its vibration. You can intend for layers of your etheric shell, or aura, to be a filter or shield. When you intend or visualize this enough times, it will eventually become part of your vibrational reality. Therefore, you can alter your etheric shell to become a more effective toxic screen around your physical and energetic body, so that nothing can reach you without being cleansed of its own toxicity. You can also use the old way of blessing your food and water and utensils with prayer or incense before you eat to purify their energy. For all things are energy, including chemicals and toxins, and can easily be transmuted through the proper intentional manipulation of said energy.

DEATH

Death is not the end, or the beginning. It is but an exhalation. A breath out. Not your last, surely, and never your first. Do you fear breathing? No. Then do not fear death, not yours or your loved one's, for it is just the exhalation of the soul. Whenever we create from the nonphysical into the physical, on any level, we inhale, or *gather*, our energies. And when we withdraw our energy from the physical, we exhale, or *release*, our energies. When a soul chooses to incarnate in the physical plane, it is like taking a very deep breath: we draw in all the energy that the universe has to offer us, and we concentrate it deeply into one point of light. This small, intense point of light is what you would call the moment of conception, the light of a cell, new life. Just as physical breath spreads the life-giving energy of oxygen through the lungs into every cell in the body, the breath of a soul catalyzes the transformation of one small cell into two, and then four, and then hundreds, and then millions. This one deep drawing in of life energy sustains all of one life. The first breath. And so, at the moment of death, the life energy is blown out, in one final exhalation: both of the soul, and the body. It is that simple. Breathe in, breathe out. You have nothing to fear. You take so very many, many breaths in your time as a soul. Why fear this one half breath, this one exhalation? And when we withdraw our energy from the physical, we exhale, or *release*, our energies. Be in love. Be in joy. In and out.

We tell you now that there is life after death and in death, that at once when you die you are alive, and reborn and alive as you have always been and never remembered when you were in physical form when you sat quietly and tried to remember you thought you did but you did not. You have not imagined the wonderful aliveness that is your very being, you have not accessed it in your waking hours. But it exists all the same. You continue forever and ever and cannot be destroyed, not a single atom of you, not one iota. Your consciousness continues and expands forever in a way that your present realm of consciousness, physical you, cannot fathom.

You think you understand this, but you do not. If you did, you would not worry about time or money or death or loss. These things are fiction, not real. You have only life, and life leads you to live.

There is more. We hear you here in our world our realm our division from you, like we have never been apart. We are not incarnated now, but we have been, and we know the difficulties you face on your world, and others on theirs. But you have chosen these realms to live in, and this is where you learn your great lessons, and create great and beautiful magics. It is where you create love and life from nothingness. Where you breathe light and feel love in every cell of your core fiber. You are light. We are blinded by your radiance, as you are when you look at the sun. We revel in your creations, and we want to help you to grow and grow, and we have promised you that we would.

We love you.

SOUL FRAGMENTS

Do souls suffer after they pass?

Souls, when they are in the light, do not suffer. Soul fragments (as opposed to the "oversoul", "higher self" or "soul anchor" that remains connected Source at all times) can perceive that they are suffering. At all times, all souls and energies are either fully in the light, or varying degrees of not perceiving their own light. There is no dark. But when one is not perceiving the light clearly, there is suffering. Souls who are stuck on earth after death, or pieces that fragment off after traumas to "hide" from the light, souls who are stuck in "limbo" or who design their own after-death purgatory, they do feel they are suffering, and their own non-light, lowered vibration, it lowers the vibration of the planes of existence around them. This is why so many lightworkers, non-physical entities and angelic realms are currently working here on earth together to help these lost souls move back into the light. As they move on, the earth lifts in vibration and can evolve.

If you are worried that a soul has not moved on, you can call in the "blue triangle beings" (see

"Night Terrors" for more comprehensive information) and your angelic guides to help you connect with him and help him move fully into the light. Connect, ask, and trust that it will be done.

JUDGMENT AND KARMA

Dear ones, why are you always judging? What is to be gained by judging everyone and everything around you? When you judge, you are not living joyously in the present moment. When you judge, you are fighting your present circumstances, and therefore focusing on what you do not want to be experiencing. This will only help you call in more of what you are not liking. When you accept everything around you, when you cease judging and open your arms to all, then the entire world will flock to you. Everything you ever wanted will appear. If you find yourself unable to do this, you must retrain your mind. Begin by disconnecting from all the energy feeds which fuel your judging. If you cannot watch American Idol without judging and appreciating all the singers and judges and songs and commercials, don't watch it for a few weeks. If you cannot watch the news without feeling badly, turn it off. If you cannot read your emails without being sad or annoyed with spam, stop checking them for a while, or install a better filter. If you cannot filter your judging, resentful emotions, let someone or something else do it for you until you can. Hand over all your negative emotions to Source. Give them to source, god, spirit, your higher self – give us your troubles, and release them. Forget about them, until the day you can remember them and wonder at why they bothered you so much. You are so blessed, you are so loved, can you not do a little of the same for the rest of the world? Begin.

Selflessness can be a wonderful act, and a great lesson, that only you can reward your Self and not to look outside the self for approval. You are the only one who is judging you. Be free and judge not. Judging others always results in one's judgement of oneself.

We would like you to know that karma is not a binding system, that you can be as free from past lives and past injuries as you want to be. You can clear your karma with pure intent in an instant, with just a strong and simple statement of WILL. We would like you to know that you do begin each life with a fresh slate, and that your memories from other lives are just that, memories. They are not part of this present moment.

Release, and be free.

HELPING OTHERS

Some people I care about seem so unawakened. I worry about how they can ascend and I am trying to help them achieve their higher purpose, help them see what they decided to work on improving in this lifetime. How can I best do this?

You cannot help them. This is their work. What you can do is be loving, and supportive, in all that they do. Their purposes are not for you to work on. You are here for you, and they are here for them. You are worried that they will not finish what they started, but you do not realize that no one ever does. Do not try to help them goal-wise, but only heart –wise. Love them. Life is not a test. It is not homework. It is recreation. It is fun. It is joy and love and all that comes in between. One cannot help another on their path because one cannot *feel* what is truly expansive or restrictive for that individual. Be in JOY, and love impeccably, honestly, and you will be honoring everyone.

SOUL GROUPS

All souls have core groups that they are in, but they move between groups, and share groups. Imagine if you were to draw three circles, all overlapping in the middle. This is how soul groups are all interconnected. So that some people from one soul group are very connected to some others in another group, and these people feel much like they are from one group. But others in the groups are not sharing this emotion, or connectedness. Only those in the overlapping areas.

When you are with someone of the same soul group, so they are more likely to remain your friend or in your life despite any differences you might have over the years. They will enjoy being in your presence and feel a slight boost to their own vibration when they are. This is normal for people in the same soul group. It does not mean that you need to be together romantically or with any degree of intensity. It can simply be beneficial to have contact, whether it is occasional or daily. When you talk or sit with a person in your soul group it helps awaken your spirit. Thus, being near members of your soul group(s) helps you heal more quickly, identify your path more easily, and receive guidance from your higher self more clearly. In many ways, you are each other's muse, their inspiration. You are good for each other.

Sometimes, soul group connections can be so intense or pleasurable that they are mistaken for romantic connection (and sometimes they are that). There is a strong sense of joy connected to being with one's soul group. It is a feeling of home. This is why it is important to be clear about what your feelings are, and where they come from.

You will feel a strong, similar connection whenever you meet someone from your soul group. In many ways they may feel like a soul mate, but it may just be the feelings of old lifetimes and connections bleeding through into your current reality. For this reason when you first meet a new person whom you are feeling this soul-connection to, we suggest that you perform a little meditation or simply state your intent quietly and firmly to yourself, to "clear and remove any all karmic ties or debris that is connected to myself and _____, and clear any past, present and future lives that might be affecting this current relationship." Once such a clearing has taken place, then you may embark on a fresh, clear relationship, without any old baggage getting in the way, or any old programs being repeated.

Who needs repeats? This life is for creation and joy, a time for new expression. Free yourself and enjoy your time wherever you are.

TWIN FLAMES

To speak of twin flames: in our reality, this is not a true phenomenon. There are many, many soul mates one can have in a lifetime, from one's soul group and also from overlapping soul groups. There are no twin flames, just as there is not just one true soul mate.

Much of the information we find on earth regarding twin flames and soul mates is very, very distorted. Twin flames are not all reconnecting right now. Twin flames are simply aspects of one soul, one spark of Source, manifesting in different bodies at the same time. It is not uncommon for humans to be incarnated in more than one body at a time, sometimes even in different times or different planets! When the souls in different bodies do meet, there is always a deep sense of connection and recognition. However, it is very rare for that connection to last long and turn into a lifelong relationship. It is simply not generally beneficial for a soul to be in a relationship with itself that way. The entire purpose of incarnating in multiple locations and dimensions is for the soul to make the most of its "time" and energy. A romantic partnership does not generally fulfill that requirement, although sometimes it can help the soul heal deep heart-centered issues. Generally, if twin flames do meet, it is for a briefer time, for the purpose of energizing both aspects of the soul and helping remind them what their purpose/mission/intent for incarnation is.

On the other hand, many "soul mates" are reconnecting now, yes. Soul mates are not actually always the perfect match for a soul. That is, again, distorted information. Soul mates are really just souls who you incarnate with frequently, who share a similar vibration and are part of your soul group. Being around them generally helps lift your vibration and increase your sense of connection and well-being. Every person has many, many "soul mates" not just one. Many of you are connecting with each other now so that you can (surprise!) wrap up old karmic patterns and release stagnant vibrations from the Earth's living matrix/the Akash/mass consciousness.

RELATIONSHIPS

When things happen easily, and joyfully, then you know that you are on the right path. When you are unhappy with someone, that is a symptom of dissonance between vibrations. Two people can be together who have very different vibrations: if they are saying yes to the others vibration, and not trying to shift their vibe or the other person's. It is this that we would like many of you to work on, to become very, very stable and secure in your own vibration so much so that no one can shake you out of it. Only then will you find the true, fantastically open and joyous love that you are yearning for. Only then will you feel truly at peace with the world. Then, dear one, miracles will begin to appear in your life, daily.

It's easy to understand that as people change, relationships also change. The mechanics of this are more difficult to live with sometimes. Sometimes I feel as if people look at me and they have to turn away. Why is it that people are sometimes seemingly repelled by an evolving soul? Can you tell me anything about the transition time where the old falls away to make room for the new? I do my best to be optimistic about these shifts, and yet I often find myself a bit lonely and confused.

When someone, or something, is not in alignment with your vibration, and you are not in alignment vibrationally with it, and you are open enough in your heart consciousness to not be concentrating on that misalignment, but rather concentrating only on those things with which you are aligned, then that someone or something will cease to be present in your reality. This is not a case of it being repelled, but of it being attracted elsewhere vibrationally. It does you no good to be surrounded by things or beings which are not vibrationally aligned with you, and it does not better them, either. All souls are evolving. To believe that one's soul is more evolved than another is always erroneous. For evolution is like a circle, and there can be no one soul that is further progressed than another on a circle. You are merely in different places on the same hoop. Souls, particles, energy: all is attracted to that which is similar to itself. Sometimes, when a soul is excited about its progress and the new things it has learned, it may try to push or attract other souls into alignment with itself: this is also an error, for souls can only be *allowed* to come into alignment. Never pushed or pulled. This is all a very natural and easy process, when one *allows* it to progress in its own time and manner. Do not push or pull. Just be yourself. Be at peace. Let your own light shine, and let the light of the world shine around you. All will be well.

GENETIC MEMORY

I believe that I sometimes experience genetic memory, and even have some skills that clearly don't derive from any study or effort in this lifetime? I feel that I can differentiate from those memories that are genetic, versus those that are from past incarnations, versus knowledge provide through spiritual connection in real time. Is this reasonable? What can you tell us about genetic memory, versus memories from past lives and versus knowledge obtained from tapping into source knowledge? How can we optimize our knowledge through these various means?

All knowledge is one. Know with your heart, and you will know what is true and what is not, what is needed now, and what is not. Use your body's physical clues. Does this knowledge make you feel good? Then it is good. Pay attention to your "gut" for it is your knowledge editor, bestowed upon you by your greater self so that you can find your way on earth.

Genetic memory is termed so because it is just that: genetic. Your DNA holds locked within it so many memories, so many secrets, that your science and reasoning cannot begin to detect or understand. The DNA of all living things shares many many strands. Do you know why this is so? We will tell you: it is because it holds within it the very instructions for translating the non-physical into the physical, all the history of all the living organisms that have ever, ever been on your planet that slowly and surely evolved into you, all the remnants of Source. All of you. You are truly ALL ONE.

Your scientists call some DNA junk. You humans are so inclined to throw away everything that you do not understand, tossing it aside, instead of simply letting it be and waiting for the day when you can and will understand it. And that is OK. It is your world, to create as you will. But know that there is NO thing in your body that is junk. No part that is not needed. Nothing obsolete. Nothing irrelevant. All is used. All is relevant. Yes, your appendix. Yes, your gall bladder. Yes, your emotions, your reason, your junk DNA, your symbiotic bacteria. Everything matters. Everything.

Ultimately, your DNA holds all the information. You can access it individually through your brain, but if you knew the proper way to read and understand this part of DNA (this is far, far off, because it is not something that is expected or believed in yet by your scientists) you would not need the brain – you would translate directly from the DNA. Your pituitary gland holds the key to unlocking all your memories, while your pineal gland allows you to actually activate your imprints, your potentials, your manifestational realities.

ALL information is available to you at ALL times, in whatever way you desire. As with everything else, you must first desire to access this information. Then you must believe that you can, and expect that you can. Whatever method works to get you to this state of being, that is how you will be able to access your information. But really, all you have to do is want it and know you can do it. Actually believe it – not just think you could maybe sometimes somehow do it if you are very lucky or in the right place at a special moment.

DNA AND THE SOUL

You are all changing, evolving. Some faster than others, each at their own pace. You are all expecting a better world, not realizing that all the while you are creating it deep within your own bodies. Some of your "junk" DNA is activating, and still more pieces of DNA and cells are changing and shifting to become something entirely new, entirely different. And yet the same, for always, always, you each carry the same divine spark of Life, of Source, of God within you. You each carry your same soul which you have always had, and without which you would not be walking or breathing, dancing or crying. Your soul was not created by the Annunaki, or the Pleiadians, or any other alien race. It was created from the same fabric of Spirit and Source energy that all matter and all space are created from. It links you to each and every spark of life in the entire universe. That is what is important, and must be remembered most of all.

BLOOD TYPES

What is the story behind RH- and RH+ blood? I've heard everything from stories about cro magnons, to reptilian aliens, to Adam and Eve...

RH- and RH+ blood represents the final splitting away of earth-humanity from its animal origins. Slowly, RH- blood is spreading. As the RH- blood becomes dominant, humanity will find itself to be less like the animal it has been, and will begin to have the abilities and characteristics of its extra-terrestrial fore-fathers, who are true humans. This is just another part of evolution, the continuation of man becoming its own species, and evolving to where it should be. At this time, there is no discernable difference between one who is RH- and RH+. The actual evolutionary changes will not be evident for hundreds of years. RH- blood at this time merely indicates the direction of mass evolution. RH+ blood holds as much ability for evolution and "special" abilities as RH- blood.

Is there a purpose for the different A, B, O, AB blood types? What do they mean?

The different blood types began at different times, as your scientists have seen. They are markers for

163

the different levels of consciousness that humanity has achieved at different times. They do NOT show if people now are more or less evolved, more or less human, or an older or younger soul. They DO indicate what priorities the person begins with in this lifetime, the issues they will be most concerned with. O types will be learning lessons about provisioning for themselves and their families. They are here to focus on family life, on root chakra issues. Their most important lessons are about how to provide for themselves with grace and ease, and in turn help humanity evolve out of survival based existence and into a state of grace and joy. A types are the builders and engineers, the ones who are finding ways to organize whatever lessons humanity is learning at the time into a manageable reality. Their challenge is often to do this in a calm and easy manner, as they often feel as if they have the entire weight of humanity on their shoulders. B types are the ones who have come in to simply enjoy life, and to harmonize the other blood types together into a cohesive, happy, mass consciousness. Their challenge is to turn the illusions of sadness of those around them into joy, to purify mass consciousness without being tainted by the lower emotions. AB types are here to bring in new ideas and new lessons. They often feel like they are outcasts and on the fringe of society, because they hold a very different reality within them than that of mass consciousness. They are the map-makers. They often feel that

164

they have arrived early, because in fact they have. Together, all the blood types are working to create a more evolved, conscious humanity. No blood type is more important or more evolved than another. They each hold a part of the key to the future.

PARENTING

Children will always benefit from seeing their parents follow their hearts. They will never have the easy courage to follow their own dreams, to fulfill their own life paths, if they have not seen adults model this behavior. Always take time to care for yourself, to walk in the light, to do what calls to your heart and fills you with joy.

ANIMAL COMMUNICATION

Lately there is much news and many videos about animals with significant ability to understand human language, make tools, choose among shapes and colors those that are different, recognize many faces, learn dressage dancing steps, sniff out cancers, etc. Why has it taken humans so long to recognize that animals are intelligent sentient beings with strong relationships, long memories and a sense of community – or are we just returning to a knowledge that humans once had in much earlier times?

Humans have long tried to differentiate themselves from the rest of the beings on your planet due to a deep-seated fear that as fellow animals they too may return to living wild. The problem has not been that man could not see how animals were like him, but that he did not want to see how HE was still like THEM.

THE AKASH

The Akash, or Akashic records, are here on our plane for all to see and access. They contain all the information of all the planes of all the times of all the beings. There is nothing we can tell you that is not in these records. They are the seamless collection of all thoughts and deeds of all conscious beings. All that has been, will be, and is, is contained in the records. They are an invisible library, the mass consciousness of the universe, of all. You can access them through your thoughts, but you do not know it. For now, if you wish, you may ask us anything and know that we have the records at our fingertips, that we and the records are one, indivisible in our non-physical reality.

PAST LIVES

When dealing with past lives, always remember that your memories have been limited for many reasons, the primary being that you wanted to learn to live in the now, fully present. Recovered knowledge from past lives can be illuminating and help you overcome certain patterns, but should be dealt with swiftly, and then let go. Not clung to. Do not allow your past lives or your ancestors to rule how you feel or how you approach your life now. It is not their time -- it is yours. As with thoughts that occur during a meditation, there should be a momentary "A-ha, so that's what that is, that is why I feel that way about XX!" and then the thought or life should be released. It is time, again, to live in the NOW.

WHY COME TO EARTH?

You want to know why you feel different, why you feel sometimes that you don't belong, and if there is more waiting for you. You wonder this especially at night, when the stars are shining and the noises outside are more quiet. And you wonder it, too, when you are with large groups of people, you wonder who are all these beings, and why are you here with them?

There are some souls who have incarnated on Earth since its own beginning. There are many who have incarnated hundreds and thousands of times. And always, there are fresh souls who are new to the planet, coming to see what all the fuss is about. Why incarnate somewhere where the beings are so limited, so massive, so physical and bound so by time? Why come somewhere where life is so busy and frail? So the souls come. It has always been so, and always will be. Know that you chose to be here so that you could experience the vast range of emotions and physical being-ness that humans experience, and bring those sensations into your soul so that you could expand and flourish.

GETTING THINGS DONE

Your endeavors as humans on earth bring us much delight in our realm. We find you very pleasing, very entertaining, as you go about creating on Earth. You are alternately very serious and very capricious. We would like you to see that one need not exclude the other. We would like you to see that though everything has importance, not everything matters. We have connected with your guides and with your greater self, and we see that this seriousness is often battling with the side of you that wants to enjoy, to have fun, to LIVE. While you have this joyous aspect of self, you also feel an urgency, like you are supposed to be doing more, doing much.

You don't realize that you already are.

You are living. You are creating. You are doing so much of what you greater self has desired for you.

The world is shifting very quickly now. Humans are raising their vibration as quickly as Mother Earth, as the animals and the trees and the stones. All are shifting. Some are shifting faster than others, but all are vibrating faster than they were a year ago, even a week ago. As your vibration rises, new possibilities, new projects, new people, will present themselves to you. Sometimes, as your vibration continues to rise, certain ideas or people will have completed their cycle with you before you feel you are "done." This is because the project or the people no longer resonate with your new vibration and with the newer ideas and progressions this brings. Later (which sometimes comes very quickly!) it may resonate once again, in a different manner. For those of you who like to complete everything they begin, this can take some getting used to.

Relax your planning. Focus only on your tasks for the day, and relax your vision so that you do not see tomorrow, or the next week. Do what you need to do TODAY. And tomorrow, do what you need to do in that day. Plan a little less, focus more on feeling good, and what comes to you will be exactly what you desire at a soul level. Your mind, your human ego, cannot plan as well as the universe can to deliver the promise of your desire. LET GO. The universe knows clearly what you want. You humans do not need to shout at it so, and wave directions in its face. We love that you do so, it is sweet and fun and good to see you so full of heart and determination, but it is not necessary.

Do not complicate matters by always *doing things*. Just be. Be you, be gorgeous, be you, be in the moment, be you, be honest, be now. Many of you used to study and speak of detachment. DO you remember that? But mostly you as a species do not practice detachment now, and that is the root of many of your troubles. You are so very invested. When something small goes wrong, it matters so much to you, it seems a major catastrophe, and then it grows and grows and grows because you are *feeding* it your attention, and then it really does become a catastrophe. If you would but turn your mind away from it and focus instead on all that is going well, you would be better off. When an organizer comes to you and says there is a complication and you must move rooms, do not worry, brush it off like a fly, and **know** that a better solution is on the way.

Be open. Be ready. Good things surround you. Every day remind yourself to open to all the wonderful ways the universe is expanding to meet your desires. Receive love, for you ARE love and what you are returns to you. Receive and BE in joy, for you are joy.

FEELING DRAINED

I am so drained right now. I am tired of being bright and happy for others. How else can I support them?

We feel your sadness emanating through all reality, and we wish that we could imbue you with all the joy that is your birthright, right here, right now. You are so blessed, and we want you to know that, feel it, believe it. You have the mistaken belief that you are there on Earth to take care of others. No no no. That is not the way. That is not why you incarnated! You went into the physical wanting to inspire and lead, to be on Earth at an exciting time of spiritual expansion and technological wonderment. You were excited that humans had gotten this far. You wanted to have friends and lovers that were creative and joyous, and to always radiate your own creative, joyous light to all those you know and love so that they could do the same right back to you.

You are that person. You do do that. But at some point you began to believe that not only must you radiate your own light, but that you must be **responsible for the light of others** as well. This self-imposed responsibility has created a heavy weight upon your shoulders, the more-so because you cannot ever possibly fulfill it. You CANNOT be the light of others. You cannot be responsible for their own creation of joy and light. You simply cannot. Each must make their own light, joy, creative happiness, love, etc. You are taking on too much now!

The only way to release your pain is to release your burden. Stop worrying about carrying others on your back. Let them carry themselves. Hold hands if you like, but only so long as you are not dragging them along, nor them you. ALL beings have free-will. All beings must be responsible for their own reality: for their own health, wealth and well-being.

The first step to change is what we call "the opening." Open your mind and heart to all possibilities. Then imagine the reality you wish you were living. You can be very specific, or more general. Put yourself "out there" and be ready for whatever may come. Do not think about the problems you have, only their positive aspects: possible solutions! See what happens. **You are a miracle maker. You can do whatever you want.** Spend some time looking around you and imagining the various possibilities, and soon opportunities will begin to present themselves.

You know what you want. You know what to do. What is holding you back is the false idea (false, because you do not believe in it, but yet you are living it) that you must subjugate your light for the good of those around you. That's not helping anyone. Let your light shine, not to cheer up others, but to cheer up you! Let your light blaze forth not because you are forcing it, but because you are **so full of joy you can't possibly hold it back**!

You are ready for change. Be it. Do it. Breathe it.

You are ready.

ECONOMIC HARDSHIP

You in your country and on your planet have surrounded yourselves with images of lack, with ideas of fear and hardship. A small percentage of you in what you call "developed" countries have ascended enough to begin to shift yourselves out of that circle of hardship, but still you fear that all will end. People talk of the end times, of global warming, of hunger elsewhere, of the poor and the stricken. Yet no one is poor, no one is stricken. They only feel so. ALL have incarnated into the areas they chose when they were but spirit, and all can arise and shift their vibration at any moment they so choose. You are, at every moment, EVERY THING. You are, at EVERY moment, able to BE anything. Fear not the lack of fossil fuel, or the rise in prices, or stricken economies, pandemic illnesses. Fear nothing. Be in JOY at all moments and always at ease, and all will continue to BE and to BECOME easy. Think of love, and it will be with you. Believe you are wealthy, for you ARE. Believe you are well, for spirit can never be anything BUT well.

I am source, as are you. We are all ONE, of one, and from one. There is no separation, and no distinction in heaven between your spirit and mine. There is no separation between having and not having. It is all one and the same, for all things exist at one and the same moment, in one and the same place, on one and the same plane. Open your eyes, and see what has always been before you. You are in the kingdom already. Eden IS now. Here. In you and around you and for always.

MAKING THE RIGHT DECISION

There is no wrong decision. This is not a test. There are no wrong choices. As many of you like to remind yourselves, "You are always in exactly the right place, at the right time, doing the right thing." We find it very amusing that you humans have to constantly remind yourself of what is such a basic truth. We are glad that you are beginning to REMEMBER this basic truth. We are even happier that many of you are beginning to LIVE this basic truth.

There is no should. It does not exist. You are not urged to do anything by the divine, nor to not do anything. The issue here is, are you happy? Are you JOY-full? Do you look forward to your days and to your nights? Release your fear of retribution, and do those things you yearn to do.

Go forward, in joy, and at peace that you are on the right path, just as you have always been on the right path. There is nothing that you can think of that you are not allowed to do, that you should not do, that you must not do. All thoughts are an act of creation, all deeds are a manifestation of creation, and all creation is

GOOD. You are good, you are whole, and it is TIME for you to be responsible to your own self and create what you desire.

Communicate with your higher self, and be that kind of selfish. Higher-selfish. Greater-selfish. Perfectly-selfish. This kind of self-ish-ness will manifest in a way that will benefit you, and in turn, all of mankind, all of earth, and all of creation.

You are loved, and you are love. Let all your thoughts go and be your self.

Be love.

We say, so many of you have been practicing.

You have been practicing what to do when you are ready to really live life. You have been waiting and waiting for the right time to live the life you were meant to, to live the life you dreamt of. You have begun many times, practicing what to do when you begin your true, destined life.

We say, you are ready now.

We would like you to know that everything you have done has been correct.

We would like you to know that everything you have experienced has had a purpose.

We would like you to know that you have accomplished much in this life, and that now, you have practiced enough.

Do you hear us? Do you understand? You **have** practiced enough. You are ready to begin.

Live your life. Be free. Do not worry that you are heavy or sloppy or disorganized. You are none of these things. Those are merely words used to distract you from the reality of who you are: You ARE a perfect being. You have spent years, minutes, days rehearsing for your life. You have been revving up, so to speak, and now, when you let your foot off the brake you will take off. Full of speed, full of energy, and full of purpose.

What is your purpose, you ask? To live! Above all, to live joyfully and to create all that you will. Joy is life. Life is joy. There is little light and love to be had in life if one is not joy-FULL.

We would like you to know that there is nothing in this world that can harm you, or that you can harm. That is important. You are all-powerful, you create your world. But you do not create anyone else's world. Only yours. And so, you cannot harm anyone else, nor can they harm you. You are a free, strong person. Claim your power.

BEING TRUE TO YOU

So often you dim your light because you are trying to match the vibration of other people, instead of staying true to your own self. If you remained true to your own self, you would not pursue relationships with people or places that are inappropriate matches for your vibration. If you remained true to the core of your being, you would not be striving to create harmony where there is none; you would always feel harmony because you would always be in a state **of** harmony.

When you dim your light, or shift your vibration, you will always become more unhappy and tired. This is because when you are following your own path and remaining true to the core of your being, your greater self, you are in a state of oneness with Spirit, and flowing with the stream of energy that is ALL. When you are **not** following your own path or remaining true to what your soul desires, you are fighting against the stream of energy that is ALL, and this is, very, very tiring to your soul and your physical being. For while you fight against yourself, you are denying pieces of your soul energy, and when you have less soul energy, you actually *have less energy.* Less to achieve your goals with. Less to make it through your day with. Less to sustain your vibratory rate with. So, when you feel sad, or tired, or angry, take a moment to think: what is it that I am doing or feeling that is not in alignment with the vibration of the core of my being? And then, try to shift your attention away from that thing, and towards something else that makes you feel lighter and happier. Continue these small shifts of attention until you reach the best feeling place you can.

Do not try so hard. Do not be so sad. You are a being of light and love, and your soul wants you to just relax within yourself and stop beating yourself up. Stop trying to create the life you want, and just let yourself BE the soul you are. The life will come of its own accord.

The only way you will ever be happy and fulfilled is to be who you are, completely. Without apologies, without reservations. Without second-guessing or looking back. Always moving forward, without needing anyone's approval. Just being truthful, open, and your own compassionate, passionate self. Becoming less reactive to other people and situations, and spending more time actively following your bliss.

For the next three weeks, as you go to sleep, try saying to yourself:

"I align with my true self and ease into the fullness of power with joy and freedom."

When you awaken, take time to savor your dreams from the night before, and say to yourself:

"I am the light of the world. I am the light of my soul. I am the power of God and good and love flows through me and around me."

Ease into your self.

You are joy.

You are light.

All will be well.

EVALUATING YOUR ENERGY

Your best work in life is to channel and express the joy of Sprit, of God or All-That-Is. It is a creative, robust job. Sometimes, many times, there are distractions.

There is nothing better to do in life than that which makes you happy. At every crossroad, you must choose what lights your fire, what kindles your spirit. And then, as you make your way towards the next crossroad, you must walk joyfully, expressing that joy, spreading your happiness while you create your reality. This is your job. This is how you are supposed to live. You are supposed to be happy. You are supposed to be a beacon of joy in the world.

How are you doing? Are you doing that? You knew what your work was when you were a child and you were very, very good at it. As you got older, you began to make decisions based more on fear – would you be accepted? Would your peers or your parents approve? Would you be safe, secure? Would you be loved? You weren't always sure anymore, and you began to choose your path based on those outcomes, rather than the simple factor – would it bring you joy? You found other ways to mimic the joy of following your heart, but they are poor substitutes. More often than now, when you live like that, you begin to feel sad or lonely. You begin to feel bored, maybe angry. Your body starts to ache, a mirror of your heart's pain.

So, let's evaluate your energy and its impact on your life's work. Are you lifting others up with your light, with your smile, with all that you create? If you are bringing people down, you are not succeeding. If the people around you are afraid to express their own joy near you, because of how you will react, you are not channeling source energy. You are doing little in the web of life as a co-creator. We know that sometimes it is hard to remember how to connect to joy, to choose love, to choose happiness.

How can you make it better, right now, today? Start smiling. Hug the people you love. Make little gestures of appreciation on a regular basis. Make big gestures, too. Choose joy. Do what makes you happy. Fight the fear monster in your head, the voice you hear at night while you lie in bed. Listen to your heart, instead.

MESSAGE FROM HUMMINGBIRD

The Deva of the Hummingbird has come today to give you a message. Do not be afraid of starting small. Small things often have more power and stamina than large things. Small things can burst into action and be full of life faster than large things. Small things are full of vigor, and joy, just as large things are, and you can grow a small thing into a large thing as easily as a large thing into a larger thing. Seeds are small, but within mere hours or days they can transform into powerful, growing plants that are more than 10 times their size. Know that anything small can do this, just as we the hummingbirds can fly farther than any other in relation to our size. Small things have the ability to hover, stationary, and take off at great speed. Do not be afraid of small things.

MULTI-TASKING VS. SINGLE PURPOSE

I have been interested in the idea of single purpose-ness, instead of multi-tasking. What is the value in this?

The value in single-tasking is that you are focusing all your will and intent on one idea or thought, and so you are empowering it with a clearer, greater burst of energy. This gives the thought a greater chance at becoming full reality, than if you are multi-tasking and not focused anywhere. However, there are different ways of multi-tasking. One can multi-task by doing many things for short bursts of time, focusing intently on each one at the time, this is the same as single-tasking. The key is to be aware of what you are thinking while you are doing something: for your thoughts and your actions should be as much in tune as possible for the greatest success.

NEWS & MEDIA

Feel at ease. Do not worry about oil prices or politics or your country. The news media has become a monster that fuels itself with bad news, rather than reporting on what is truly happening. They need bad news, so they inflate it. More people need to go outside and watch less television. TV is something that controls mass consciousness, and it is, in general, directed by those of lower vibration, thereby when you watch it, especially the news, the crime shows, the murder shows, the talk shows, your vibration also lowers because the primary vibration on mainstream TV is one of *fear.* We are not saying you must get rid of your TV but you humans should be more discerning of what you do and do not watch. Your children, especially, should be monitored more closely, for the lower vibrations it fills them with can override the purer vibrations they entered with.

Do not fear any future. Life will continue to improve. The forces of fear and darkness would like you to succumb to their drama, but it is only a game, only a play, and not real. They cannot win.

The reality is that everyone is progressing rapidly on an evolutionary scale and there is no reason to be worrying so much about the present because there is no longer any such thing as a status quo: change is occurring rapidly, every moment, and nothing is lasting long enough to be worried about.

DOOM & GLOOM PROPHECIES

So many prophecies from before 2012 talk of many disasters to befall the earth and humanity. Some seem to be happening now, such as layoffs, foreclosures and weather patterns. I just recently found another website predicting widespread upheaval and disaster on the Earth in the next few years. It's far from the first time I've seen such fear inspiring information and it seems to affect many. It's obvious our Earth and her people are experiencing changes, it's just I've always believed these changes to be for the better rather than for destruction. Can you please shed some light on these gloom and doom prophecies? What do you say of our future?

These prophecies you speak of are of the old ways. They are often accurate from their perspective in time. But the future changes all the time. There is no true "future" to see as you humans think of it, only the present, and the present possibilities or likelihoods. So their present possibility has not become YOUR present possibility. Humanity has created a whole new host of present possibilities. Most are much more favorable to survival and JOY than before. Humans worldwide are bringing in more joy every day. Some areas of the world are not excelling at this, but they are trying to catch up, and those that do not will simply fall behind, and fall away.

Is the phoenix rising? Is the earth shifting? Is humanity evolving into a new reality? Yes, yes, YES! There will still be new wars and some accidents as were spoken of, but the days of mass Armageddon have fallen away to the past, and now much smaller losses of life are expected by those that watch the earth. And we see that every day those too are shrinking. We see that the Earth is no longer in a position where she and her creatures will have to experience such a traumatic upheaval in order to shift to a new, better reality. Right now, the earth is shifting vibrationally at a rate never before seen in this universe. Beings from all stars and planets are coming to watch. Non-physical entities are coming to watch. We are all watching, and learning. Some beings, it is true, work with the fear that some humans possess and try to augment that fear, not from a place of evil, but because they do not possess the ability to *feel* themselves, and fear is such a strong emotion that they believe they may perhaps be able to feel it if they strengthen it in others. This has not worked. Nor can they feel love, not yet. But do not fear these beings, for you are stronger than any of them, as are all humans. You have immense capacity for love. Jesus and those of his family were all but humans, and they all were able to achieve miracles beginning to be able to do this. To return to your question, we believe that the catastrophic changes predicted by some are no longer going to occur. Yes, there will still be wars, and natural disasters, until the earth has finished shifting to her new vibration, but there will be no Armageddon. That was old information, based on the old rate of ascension that humans were experiencing, then, humans simply were not accelerating fast enough to outpace the destruction they were causing. But now, they are, and it is something few expected possible, because it has never happened this way before. Some people are still tapping in to the old information. And some people are being guided by entities based in fear – this is where new prophecies of fear and mass destruction are coming from. Do not fear your life, all will be well. Life is improving. Often you humans take a step back for every two steps forwards, but still, you are progressing.

Live as if all is well, because all **is** well. If you live as if there is a crisis, then you will be one of those beings who is helping the world to create a crisis. If you live in fear, then you are creating fear. If you live in sorrow, you are creating sorrow. If you live in joy, you are creating joy. Which would you like to create? Your energy is like a stone thrown in a pond. It ripples throughout your community, throughout the world, affecting everyone and everything. When you are sad or fear-full, your energy spirals downwards, and your entire face and demeanor change. Everywhere you go, subtle and not-so-subtle body and voice signals let others know you are miserable. And the downward spiral of your energy tugs on all but the strongest of souls, pulling their energy down, and casting a mist of fear or sadness upon them as well. And then they spread this fear too, and so on, and so on. Fear, sadness, misery, hopelessness, these are all debilitating, viral emotions. But did you know that joy, hope, confidence, and expectation are also viral emotions? Wouldn't you rather germinate these emotions in others? Would you not prefer to plant seeds of joy that will spread and grow throughout the world? This is where the phrase "Be the change you want to see in the world" leads you. Throw a stone of hope or joy, and see where those ripples lead to. Be ever vigilant of what stones you are throwing in your pond. There will be "disasters" this month. There will be places where people die suddenly, and other places where more fighting breaks out. But there will be so many more places where love and compassion are spreading and expanding. Your news people may not report these places, because they do not know how to recognize "news" when it is positive. But it will be happening. Look for love wherever you go, and be like a gardener, help it grow.

All is well.

Do not fear your future.

MORE ON THE NEW EARTH

There have already been some major, large shifts in how humans live from day to day, how they behave to one another. There will be more minor tragedies, some more terrorism and shootings. The United States will have some small revolutions and evolutions and business on a day to day level will shift ever so slightly, as people at all levels of society begin to manifest the ideal of "pay it forward" with exponential results. There is already more love and much less fear throughout the world. People have changed without even realizing it. Many have not even noticed the shift, because it will seem as if always there was this love in their hearts. Some people who are not of love and light will "check out". Not all dying, but many seeming to quietly disappear from the lives of those who are of love. As those of love shift up to the new Earth vibration, so those not of love will be shifted out of their daily lives, out of their world. Technology will change very, very quickly, so much so that there is no point even trying to keep up with it, simply flow with it and follow the leads of the young. Those in need of sustenance and shelter will find what they need more easily. Those in need of money will receive abundance more easily. Everything will begin to flow in ways they have not for the last 20 years. Darker minds will try to keep the people in fear by spreading stories of hate and separation, but the stories will fade over time, and become meaningless in a world that is ruled by love. Those who stay stuck in the dark will not be able to fool the world for long, and many will lose their positions of power over it. Those who are sick and in pain will need to choose whether they stay with the fear, with the dis-ease, or if they move forward into the new loving energies. The new energies of love on the planet will be able to wash away all pain and chronic illness with ease for all those with open hearts. Doctors will eventually need to embrace a new paradigm of medicine, one of love and upliftment, support and clearing, or else they will be left without work. This will slowly become obvious to them over the coming decade. We promise you, time will bring great changes. We promise you, there is much planning for joy and evolution. The stage has been set and everything is already in motion, so try as anyone might, this evolution into love cannot be stopped. Embrace love, embrace yourself, and follow your heart to joy!

RIGHT & WRONG

There is an awakening going on. You know that.

Do you also know that everything you think you know is wrong?

And do you also know that everything you believe is right?

Do you understand that your concepts of right and wrong, good and bad, are not mutually exclusive?

ALL is one. ALL is the same. ALL is part of source. You still do not see that, you truly don't. And do you understand that lack of seeing, lack of understanding is OKAY? You are in this world, right here, right now, to **live!** You are here now to be just as you are. Nothing you desire is bad. Nothing you hate is wrong. Everything is the same. This is why the Buddhists speak of detachment. This is why Christ tells you to judge not. Attachment, judging: these are a waste of time and of energy. BE. Believe. Be alive! That's it. That is the tall order of the day. THAT is why you incarnated. Your experience, every little bit of it, is feeding source, fueling the creative power of all that is. Source wants you to want, source wants you to continue to desire and be joyful, for when you do, you are creating more of your self for you, for source, for all.

RACISM

Why does skin color create such difficulties and divisions, so much still to overcome?

Everyone is overcoming something. Each soul here on earth is working towards an evolutionary goal. Each goal is highly personal, and chosen before the soul incarnates on earth. The situations that many people are going through publicly help to raise the consciousness of the planet by shining light on issues that ALL need to resolve. Others are working on more personal issues. Do not fall into the trap of believing that anyone is a victim, or that any soul is working through more than another. There is no order of lessons. All lessons are the same. All evolution is the same. Everyone benefits from each aspect that is overcome or released. Even those souls who came here with little karma and planning to "raise consciousness" have their own sets of issues to work through. Everyone is wrapping up karma. Right now, it is the people with darker skin in your nation that are still releasing issues of disparity and slavery. But at other times it has been the whites subjugating the whites, or other races abusing others. Humanity still has work to do, and everyone is pitching in!

WHAT IS RUIN?

What is ruin? Is it the loss of all material security and resources? Or it the paralyzing fear that straps one in place? Does ruin exist when a home is lost, and the opportunity to begin fresh and anew comes? Does ruin exist when all one's limbs are gone, or when life ends? No. It does not. There is no such thing as ruin. Death is not the end. Losing material possessions is not the end. Many of the most successful business people have lost it all, begun again, and built something even better. Even more have repeated that process **more than once**. The only agent of ruin is fear. Life is only wasted when it is not lived to its fullest. It is not wasted when there is a business failure. It is not wasted when there is a physical or emotional setback. It is only wasted when you shrink into yourself and take no action, when nothing is done, because the outcome is unsure, daunting, or "scary." That is the surest way to ruin a life.

RESISTANCE

There is such a great proliferation of love and light right now on your planet. A few bodies are still pushing the fears, pushing the lies, but no one is really buying it anymore. The mass consciousness of humanity on earth is really and truly well beyond that now. Racism, intolerance, hate, these things are all being less accepted. The universal law of silence has been repealed, and now the truth is coming to light. Truth, honesty, compassion. These are the new golden rules that are shining forth from humanity, rewritten in mass consciousness for all to know.

Some are more resistant to others to the changeover. This is not because they are bad people or less advanced than you. No. Their souls have agreed to do this, to play this part now, so that all of humanity can move forward. By consciously having something to move against, by seeing what it is that must end, it is made ever so much more clear how to move forward. We are now in the final patterns of emergence. Like a butterfly, you are breaking out of your casing. Your souls are shining through and you are be-coming Christ-consciousness on earth. Use this time now, wherever you are, to engender more fully those aspects of beauty and change your wish to see fulfilled in your world. Speak you truth. Be who you are. Be wonder-full. Encourage others to do and be the same. Not the same as you, but the same as their souls. BE the light. You are light. Your body actually shines, producing its very own measurable photonic light rays. Increase the light in the world and brighten up your corner of the earth.

Please know that the souls of the bodies that are pushing negative messages are not lower vibration or lagging behind in any way. No. You should honor and adore these people because their souls have agreed to do the final work of coalescing humanity into mass agreement for a new age, a new world order. Not a world order of greed and control, but a true grass roots movement of joy and redemption, of compassion, empathy and love. These souls are helping humanity cleanse itself by shining a light on the small seeds of fear and doubt which still remain. So no, do not hate them. Do not let them make you angry.

Smile when you hear double-talk, laugh when you hear a lie: for you know that it is driving all of you towards truth, towards beauty and light. No longer are the masses taken in by old patterns. So many of you have awakened. It is a true revolution on earth, one that is still in its infancy, but it is global, make no mistake. The tide has turned, and billions of humans are completely turned on, tapped in to Source, delighting in its glory, taking up the sword of truth. Discrimination is becoming the exception, not the rule. Abundance is spreading. People are sharing their wealth and their warmth. Everyone is opening up to new experiences, in little ways, in big ways. The world is becoming lighter. You are becoming lighter.

So, now, what can you do to further this growth? How can you help bring the world closer to this glorious new age? Begin with your self. Shine your light on everything around you. Spread only truth. Celebrate only joy. Light up the world.

Your soul is pure radiance – lighten the load so that your body and mind can join with your soul in full harmonic resonance.

Support physical health with fresh produce, supplementing whichever nutrients you may be lacking. Do some juicing in the morning, or cut out some of the processed foods in your kitchen. The closer your dinner is to the original state of a food, the higher in life-giving energy it will be. You simply cannot function as full radiant being in this physical reality if your body is lagging behind.

Boost your self up with flower essences, homeopathics, reiki, whatever vibrational remedies and life energy modalities you feel comfortable with, whatever makes you feel even a little bit more excited, more eager to face the day.

Get outside for 10-20 minutes a day and give yourself a dose of sun energy. Your body is constantly emitting low levels of light, measurable quantities of photons, yes you, star that you are. Recharge your body and soul with some source-star energy and you'll feel even better. UV light kills germs and is a vital source of vitamin D. It brings you all the colors of the rainbow, energizing you on a quantum level.

Initiate all the systems of your being. Activate, align, balance, clear and connect all your chakras on a regular basis, on all 12 levels of the body, all 12 strands of DNA. Make sure that the energy from source is being properly stepped down into your physical body and that it is fully integrating and fueling your daily actions. Check in with your aura, clearing and smoothing any disturbances.

Work with your merkaba – make sure that it is fully loaded, shining and spinning. When it's running properly it is a vortex of manifestation, an energetic computational machine which interacts directly with source to create the reality you are wanting. If you haven't consciously programmed it, it's not creating much of anything.

You are beings of infinite creation.

There is very little in this universe that you yourself cannot do. Today the question is, what did you come here to do? Are you living your joy? Are you connecting with your true self, with all of you that IS? Are you ready to move forward and co-create as reality that follows you dreams?

Step forward, little one. Step forward, brave one. Step forward, and shine bright.

You are the future of this earth. You are creating a blueprint for future generations – you are experimenting for god, for all of Source: how can a physical soul be present, be vibrating highly and yet be still at the same time. How can one ascend and yet be physical at the same time? You are processing many, many different scenarios for all of source, for all of us, for ALL that IS, at this time. You are doing immense co-creative work. You will get there. You are getting there. You are all key figures. Continue.

FREEDOM

Independence is lauded as freedom from tyranny and repression, as liberation. We would like you to take this moment to look deeply within yourself and your community and see – what freedom is still lacking? What do you repress in yourself, out of fear of being judged by others? Many of you say you have freedom of speech, but what do you refrain from expressing because of your fear of retaliation from peers and family? How free are you, really?

Opening up to a greater level of heart-centered living and loving means that you need to love all aspects of your self first. If you are repressing aspects of your self, then you are passing judgment on yourself. You cannot pass judgment on yourself and not pass judgment on others. This is not possible. Thus, when you are fearful and repressing yourself, you are not living in a heart-centered way. You are living in the old paradigm, centered in the solar plexus circling the old dichotomy of fear vs. joy.

Today, claim your freedom. Speak your truth. Dress how you want to. Admit to yourself what it is you are really wanting and not wanting. Look deeply into the well and gaze upon your true reflection. Only then will you know true freedom.

ASTROLOGY

I recently requested a comprehensive and computerized astrological psychological reading. It was amazing. I don't understand how a computerized reading system like this can be so accurate. It certainly makes me believe that the science of astrology can be very precise and accurate when done by a skilled practitioner. Could Eden shed some light on whether astrology was created by Source to provide these insights? I'm curious if all of this astrology was created before there were humans wanting an analytical framework for assisting in our free choices and our understanding of ourselves, or whether it evolved through the desires of humans or other analytical beings from other places. I realize we have free choice, but wonder if this is provided for us to use as part of the framework of our choices and the framework for the physical aspects that we came into in our incarnation.

You come into the world as a physical being with an unlimited connection to your higher self and Source. Over the course of human physical history, man has become more shielded from Source information by the imprints of mass consciousness: Although you are born with full connection, you quickly adjust to the same level of connection as your parents and mass consciousness in general, which means, at this time, that there is not nearly as much communication between your physical consciousness and Source as there should be. You know that you have the "emotional guidance system" of which so many speak, allowing your emotions to at least offer some direction. This was created at the same time as physical incarnation. And, so, was astronomy and astrology. The two coexist and evolved together simultaneously. For the universe itself has NOT disconnected itself from source. Its patterning and design is plainly exposed for all to see, to read, to understand, to know. It does not hide from itself. And as IT (the universe) is one with Source, and as YOU one with source, so are you one with it. Which means that your pattern and plans and desires and inclinations are also plainly written there for all to see... if they know how to look.

So, no, humans did not create astrology. It merely IS. The information exists because you and the stars are one, because you and source are one, because source and the stars are one. If you knew how, you could read the same information in the light of the sun, the wind, the plants, the flow of the river, the sound of silence. **Anywhere. Everywhere**.

The science of astrology, the ability to read the stars, humans re-opened, re-developed, re-activated, that ability because they were dissatisfied with their disconnection from Source. They yearned to reconnect. And so the early pioneers of connectivity developed dream walking, astrology, shamanic techniques, and other "magic." These were not "new abilities" but rather a reawakening. And there is SO much more, human! Still, with all this progress, you are barely connected as a group. But everyday more are reconnecting, and developing greater understanding of their true selves and potentials.

The newer computer programs that have been developed are accurate in their divinations because they are merely "computing" the data that the universe is putting forth. They are as good or as bad as the astrologers that design them to begin with. If the astrologer who designs a program has deep insight and understanding when reading a conjunction or a planetary position, and records it properly in the computer program, then the program will forever be endowed with the same height of understanding and insight. This is not magic. This is science being used to translate Source information for the human mind.

DREAMING

All are dreaming. Dreaming their reality, and their in-reality. Everyone has had the ability to enter the real worlds and dimensions of their dreams, but in recent years the ability has grown, progressed. This is a natural result of the raising of vibration of the planet. As Gaia shifts and raises her dream, so too will the animals, the plants, even the humans. As your night-dreams become more potent, so will the power in daytime to potentize, to activate ones desires and day-dreams. More than ever, the power to create is within you all.

Many of you are dreamwalkers, healers, and you have come to this planet to be a light in the dark (though more and more lights are turning and on, and so the planet is ever less dark, and ever more bright), and you are succeeding in every way that your soul, your greater self, imagined before you were birthed. Often, you are very active during the dreamtime, though you do not remember all your dreams. At night, you are often traveling, healing others on your earth and also visiting other worlds and dimensions. You are inter-galactic healers, and lately, you have been much in demand. This can leave you feeling a little more

tired than usual when you awaken in
morning. When you fall asleep at night, if you
you need extra rest, say out loud to yoursel
intend to sleep well tonight and regenerate bo
my body and soul. Tonight, I intend to stay ne
my body, and use this time simply to reenergiz
and receive messages which are beneficial to me
in this reality, on this plane of existence." You can
vary the words. Simple statements like this signal
your mind and body what they are to do, so that
you can both sleep and dream consciously and
with intent. You can also *intend* to dream when
you want to, dream how you want to.

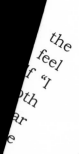

TERRORS &
HAUNTINGS

...ing night terrors and I feel presences in the ... It's physically painful and I can feel them ...ch my feet. The next day I wake up in pain. I ...so have nightmares. It's beginning to wear me down. Is this kind of thing common when you are developing? I have tried protecting the room and myself before going to bed but it isn't working.

What you are experiencing is certainly not a necessary "step" in one's development or spiritual unfolding. Part of what is happening is that souls which you were connected to in a past life are connecting to you once again, and while they are not inherently evil (there is no such thing) nor do they mean you harm, their vibration is no longer compatible with yours and so they are creating severe disharmony in your environment, your body and your psyche. They are merely trying to connect with you again, but it is bringing up memories which you do resonate with anymore, and their vibration is so different than yours that your energetic body finds itself exhausted and in pain after each of their attempts.

What you have been lacking in your own attempts to keep the room clear is both *conviction* and *intent*. You do not really believe that you have the power to banish any presence from your reality. You do not believe that you, always, have the power. Nothing can harm you or remain in your presence unless you allow it. You are the creator of your reality, and you have the power to remove these souls from your reality. And now that you have a clearer idea of who and what these beings are, we are confident that you can and will make the next leap to simply instructing them to leave.

In the meantime, we would like to introduce you to the *Sweepers* and the *Blue Triangle Beings*. The Sweepers are a collection of angels that you can visualize with large brooms who literally come in and "sweep" a room, energetically clearing it of any and all disharmonious energies or beings that do not "belong" there. The blue triangle beings are actually lightworkers harnessing their merkabas to work together with non-incarnated beings on the astral plane: they help the deceased and those of other dimensions pass along to their next point of light, to return to the place they are most in vibrational alignment with. They clear the earth's atmosphere of the soul debris left by the many souls which are choosing not to reincarnate again on earth. This clearing is helping lighten and lift Earth's vibration. They are available to all people, at all times, you simply need to call them in and ask them to remove the being or soul which is bothering you and take it to where it needs to go. Some souls require more convincing than others – the process can take anywhere from moments up to several weeks.

I have evil spiritual entity's that are around me. How do I get rid of them?

Intention is everything. The method does not matter. What matters is your attention and your focus. There are many ways to cast them out, but with each method you must understand that you are the supreme power in your reality. You determine what can and cannot be in your space. You determine what is allowed to siphon off your aura (nothing should!) You determine who and what can connect with you.

Use whatever tools you like to clear your space and focus your intention and state with authority that you are casting these entities into the light. There is no place for them here, they do not belong in this dimension, and you send them with love into the fire of creation, into the light of source. In reality, there is no such thing as evil beings, only beings which operate on a different frequency than you and interact poorly with your energy field. This is because they truly do not belong in your physical realm, and must return to source to be returned to their own true homes.

Tools you might use for clearing are smudge, incense, candles, singing bowls, drums, rattles, bible psalms, etc. Salt around the boundaries of the home helps bring in the earth element and clear and protect the space. Black tourmaline and selenite carried on your person will help keep you clear until your aura is stronger.

FLYING

My dreams of flying are so real and so often that I feel that I can fly. Many people say that flying is an out of body experience. But to me, it feels very different than projecting oneself out of the body on a journey to another place. I have not had the sense of flying during non-dream time, but I hold the belief that I can fly. Is there any value in trying to manifest flying in non-dream time?

There are as many ways of flying as you can think of. They are all valid and equal. Different people choose to fly different ways. Few choose to fly these days in your reality. This is all due to fear. You can fly if you want to, but it takes great belief and great expectation. There is value in ALL that you choose to manifest. No manifestation is more valuable than the next. Create and be joyful, that is what you came here to do. If flying will bring you joy there is great value in that. Flying in your reality would also show you the truth that you can create all that you wish to manifest. That belief would be more valuable than anything else.

META HUMANS

I hear that there is still much research going on by various government military organizations into psychic ability. Is it true and does this research moving in a direction that can eventually benefit the planet? Does Eden have some insight to this?

By searching for psychic phenomena, psychic phenomena is being created. Everything that one wants to find or hopes to find is eventually created and manifested on your plane. Soon, you will have free energy. Soon, you will have witches who can fly. Soon, you will have optimal weather everywhere. So it is with the studies of the government, which mirror movies and books in your culture. Your culture has a predominant yearning at this time for psychic abilities in people, and so they are manifesting on spectacular levels. Your culture yearns for super heroes. These, too are not far behind.

TECHNOLOGY

Be well. Be joy-full. Technologies have been evolving to heal the world's vehicle consumption of fuel. And more new technologies are arriving. Much is changing now. Many scientists are downloading information in their sleep from other planets and realms, even from their future selves, about what they can do to heal the planet through their area of expertise.

CRYSTAL SKULLS

What do crystal skulls do? Who do they connect with? Are they beneficial?

All crystal skulls are not the same. The different crystals that they are made with carry different vibrations and energies. But all skulls, no matter who they are made by, connect to and carry the same vibration of the first skulls, who came from the ancients. Originally the skulls were used as communication devices, and to waken the DNA of early humans so that they could evolve. Now, the new modern skulls also awaken the DNA, the bodies and minds of all humans. They help you change. You worry that perhaps you are connecting to aliens who do not have your best interests at heart? You are not. The skulls connect only to your higher self and the truth of your DNA. They do nothing that is not already given or asked for in your genetic coding. They merely tap into your true self, the billions of reams of "junk" DNA and brain cells that you do not use, so that you can become a fuller expression of who you are meant to be. Each crystal skull also carries with it the personality or spirit of its original stone piece.

ALIENS

I recently had contact with a woman whose is working closely with "the grays", alien lifeforms, without realizing it. I saw that she was missing certain chakras and organs which have been stolen by them. It seemed very sinister to me. Who are these grays, really? How could a human invite them in to their experience?

How indeed? How does a person invite a murderer into their experience, an abuser, or a car crash? There are always lessons to be learned. Sometimes the invitation to learning extends from a moment far in the past, even from another lifetime or an ancestor.

You are all infinite beings, and you are expanding on all levels all the time. Some of you, in your earthbound need for variety and contrasting situations, are contracting instead: decreasing your energy. This sort of energy can be recognized easily in victims and the abused. The grays are creative beings which are on a different harmonic level, and have learned to use the creative energy from other beings in other realities to augment their own creative experience. They view the creative process without joy, in a very scientific manner, and are constantly trying to learn more about it. For this reason, they are particularly drawn to humans, who are some of the most creative beings in the universe.

The Grays are not bad or evil, as there is no real thing such as bad or evil. It is merely what it is. A learning experience. When a human is having contact with the grays it does not benefit them energetically, but eventually they learn to recognize this and that is when it becomes a valuable lesson in learning to differentiate between expansion and contraction. The best way to help such a person is to augment their energy in such a way that they can learn the lesson faster. If you find that their gray-linked energy is distracting or harmful to your own creative experience, then you must create a new reality for yourself where their energy cannot co-mingle with yours, whether that means removing yourself from their life or merely creating a protective bubble around your home so that all gray energy must be "checked" at the door.

WE THE PLEIADIANS

We the Pleiadians are ready to speak with you now. When you speak directly with us you may feel how our voice comes in stereo at both temples. It is a slight pressure you feel and it is because of the temporal shift involved in speaking with us. You are at that time slightly out of sync with the world, which is why it is hard for some of you to remember our messages. We talk to many of you in the night, in the dreamtime, the astral. What have we said to you in the night? We are coming. We are coming for you. For all of you. We are coming to hold you in the night and we are coming to see you through the dark times as the light emerges. There will be no alien apocalypse. There will be no massive global disaster or water rising in a dangerous way. Everything will be averted. All will be well. Some of you WILL leave this planet. Yes. Some in the guise of violent crimes are already leaving. Some in the guise of natural death are leaving. There will also be conscious suicides and some designed death. It will not hit those in the Pleiadian families, unless they want to go. There are many in these families, and there are some who are not. But no one leaves unwillingly.

Those of you who connect strongly with Jesus are connecting with us, a "recent" lineage, for who you call Jesus was actually one of our leaders who stayed behind. If you connect with crow, know that often it is showing you that the ability to shapeshift is part of DNA technology that we have left inherent in your bodies. You starseeds, you shifters of humanity, are capable of far more than you can imagine. Crows are from our planet, our terra firma, we brought them to earth with us much like you would bring dogs or cats. They carry much knowledge in their family, too. Those who feel an affinity for them are part of our family. Those who fear them, who fear the birds, are from the reptilian nations or have signed contracts with the other nations. Know that as a soul you can choose your lineages before you incarnate, and activate the strands you desire in your DNA.

ANGELS

What is the difference between angels, cherubim, or seraphim?

This is another example of getting caught up in definitions and orders from another's reality. We are all one. And yet we are all unique. As there are many many peoples on your planet, shapes and sizes, beliefs and desires, there are also different color of souls, sizes of angels, everyone chooses as they WILL, when they will. Desires change often, and everything is constantly changing. Do not worry so much about categories, for no souls or energies stay one way for very long. We all evolve, and change, and flux, and yet we all are the same, and we are all one, and from one, and to one.

In your question, all are angels. Different sizes, at different times, and none exist the same way that they did when those words were created. You can read books referring to the ancient texts, but it is better not to focus upon the past when you strive towards the future.

ARCHANGELS

The Archangels are high-level energetic beings, very connected to Source energy, who never incarnate on earth as a human, though they have shown themselves often enough over the eons to humans, and they are capable of gathering their energies so that they have mass and appear as matter. They watch over Earth as stewards, caretakers, the ultimate guides and helpers. Like workers at an information booth, they are always available to lend a helping hand.

Archangel Michael is available to all beings at all times to everyone for protection, strength and guidance. He is one of the best known archangels, very powerful and well-loved by many. Call on him whenever you feel like you need some extra strength or fortitude, when you need some "ooomph" in your step, when you need to clear a space or are feeling vulnerable.

VAMPIRES

It seems much of our society is presently engaged in a fascination with vampires at this time. Through television and movies stories surrounding these creatures seem to be everywhere. Is there any insight as to what may be the reason behind this particular trend?

At this time on your planet there is an awakening. The hidden aspects of spirit are being brought to light, fears are being released and revealed. The majority of vampire texts and stories emerging at this time are showing both the light and dark aspects of this being, a being which does exist on other planes of Earthly reality, but not in yours as it is generally portrayed. The value of this lesson is that it is now being shown that vampires, man's only natural predator on Earth, are not inherently evil. Many are good in these stories. The fact that they must subsist on blood is part of their physical nature, and not in itself evil, just as the fact that most human bodies require the intake of animal flesh is not evil. The cougar who eats the rabbit is not evil. It is merely living as it was designed to do. Clearly, there is a manner of killing, for all animals, that is in balance with earthly nature, and a manner which is out of

228

balance. And here in these stories of vampires we have vampires which kill for sport and cruel amusement, and vampires who kill only to feed or as necessary. Animals, unless ill or out of vibrational alignment with their true being, only kill to sustain themselves, not for sport, and never because they are "mean."

Humans, at this time on earth, are also learning to kill humanely: both through the global investigation and implementation of humane and ethical livestock management and with the ever-increasing trend towards global peace and warfare that sheds proportionately less civilian blood than ever before.

Vampire stories in general also mirror and illuminate the dark memories of man from times when you fed on one another for sustenance and power, as well as when you fed on your near-relatives the Neanderthals to the point of their extinction. Only miniscule traces of their blood remains, mixed with modern human blood, from the inter-species spouses who survived quietly here and there. The stories also highlight human fears of all alien entities, both good and bad, seen and unseen. You sense the existence of extra-dimensional beings, and because you cannot see them, they are doubly feared. Yet none of these entities are evil – they merely do not belong in their world. Harbor them not, but fear them not. Entertain them not, but hate them not. They belong in your world no more than you belong in theirs. You are of different realms, and in different vibrations. That is all.

PLANETARY ASCENSION

The light and the love that surrounds the planet right now is astounding. Everywhere, on all planes, coalitions of beings are coming together to stream greater amounts of love and light into the etheric blueprint of the Earth. People are doing it. Angels are doing. The elementals are doing. Off-worlders and non-physical beings are doing it. The influx of love and light energies that are pouring into the planet are expanding and increasing each day, as love and light attracts more of the same. You see terror and fear and hate and intolerance and ask, *but how can this be true?* And we say unto you that it is indeed true, and that the coming years will bring to your planet a marked decrease in fear. A decrease in suffering. Yes, there will be events that shake you in your boots and try to make you believe in the strength of the dark. But there will be love, always love, in such great quantities that we tell you: all will be well.

Remember: there is no dark. There is only the perception of the dark. All dwell in the light and the love of Source, and it is only the perceived disconnection from the light that causes an experience of the dark. With this perception come suffering, and there have been those on your planet who have tried their worst to shroud the Earth in shadow – but no more. Beings from all realms have had enough, and are with you. The earth is armored in amounts of lights and love that are unprecedented before this day. And so we remind you: ALL IS WELL.

Do you not believe it? Repeat with us: All IS Well.

The light is here. Source blesses you from every angle. From above and below, from without and within. You are blessed. Do not dwell in fear. Remember, always, that love is here. And it is winning the day. The battle between love and fear, light and dark, is over. We are now in the reconstruction period. Love is here. Light is here.

THERE ARE NO ENDINGS

Today is a great day. It is a beginning day. It is an ending day. It is a day for you to take a breath and release all the fears you hold at this moment. Just this moment. And now breath in and receive all the divine blessings of Spirit, of the Universe, of you essential being, which surround you. You are a divine spark of light in the universe. Shine your light for the world to see. Let it radiate from within you. Be as a flame which attracts the moth: do not seek the moth, it will seek you. When you unveil your true light, all that you desire and love returns to you. The brighter your light, the faster they will come. Be true. Be honest. Be Joy-FULL. Be YOU. All will be well. You are a bridge between heaven and earth – stay connected to both. Allow the sky and the earth to feed your soul. Don't forget to look up, and around, as you live your day.

You are expanding and growing, and it is a wonderful thing to behold. You are human in every way, creating and living and loving.

Bless you,
Eden

ADDITIONAL INFORMATION

More messages and personal readings
from Eden are available online at
www.edenisnow.com

MORE FROM EARTH LODGE

Shamans Who Work with The Light
Simple and Natural Herbal Living
Natural Animal Healing
Equine Herbs and Healing
Energy Healing for Animals
The Comprehensive Vibrational
Healing Guide
Conversations with Stones
Palm Reading for Everyone
Practical Reiki Symbol Primer
The Girls Who Could Series
Grounding and Clearing
Magical Mudras
Lost & Faerie Found
A Child's Collection of Rumi
Number, Name & Color
Shades of Valhalla
Fates of Midgard
Gifts of Elysielle
Song Walker
The Warping

96337915R00147

Made in the USA
Lexington, KY
19 August 2018